FREEDOM

Peak District

EASTERN MOORS AND THE SOUTH

Peak District

EASTERN MOORS AND THE SOUTH

Roly Smith

Series editor Andrew Bibby

FRANCES LINCOLN

FREEDOM TO ROAM

The Freedom to Roam guides
are dedicated to the memory of
Benny Rothman

Frances Lincoln Ltd
4 Torriano Mews
Torriano Avenue
London NW5 2RZ
www.franceslincoln.com

First published by Frances Lincoln 2005

British Library Cataloguing in Publication Data
A catalogue record for this book is available from the British Library

ISBN 0-7112-2498-6
Printed and bound in Singapore by Kyodo Printing Co.
9 8 7 6 5 4 3 2 1

Frontispiece photograph: Derwent Edge

Contents

Acknowledgments

The author would like to express his sincere thanks in particular to Gill Millward, Countryside Access Improvement Officer for Derbyshire County Council, for her vital and most willing help in obtaining copies of the elusive 'conclusive' area maps. Also to my good friends Terry Howard of SCAM, Roger Redfern of Brampton and Ray Manley for his, as ever, magnificent photography; Mike Rhodes, Access Officer for the Peak District National Park, for checking the routes; Rob Morris and Mel Capper at the Countryside Agency and, last but not least, Andrew Bibby for asking me to write the book.

Series introduction

This book, and the companion books in the series, celebrate the arrival in England and Wales of the legal right to walk in open country. The title for the series is borrowed from a phrase much used during the long campaign for this right – Freedom to Roam. For years, it was the dream of many to be able to walk at will across mountain top, moorland and heath, free of the risk of being confronted by a 'Keep Out' sign or being turned back by a gamekeeper.

The sense of frustration that the hills were, in many cases, out of bounds to ordinary people was captured in the song 'The Manchester Rambler' written by one of the best-known figures in Britain's post-war folk revival, Ewan MacColl. The song, which was inspired by the 1932 'mass trespass' on Kinder Scout when walkers from Sheffield and Manchester took to the forbidden Peak District hills, tells the tale of an encounter between a walker, trespassing on open land, and an irate gamekeeper:

> He called me a louse, and said 'Think of the grouse',
> Well I thought but I still couldn't see
> Why old Kinder Scout, and the moors round about
> Couldn't take both the poor grouse and me.

The desire, as Ewan MacColl expressed it, was a simple one:

> So I'll walk where I will, over mountain and hill
> And I'll lie where the bracken is deep,
> I belong to the mountains, the clear running fountains
> Where the grey rocks rise ragged and steep.

Some who loved the outdoors and campaigned around the time of the Kinder Scout trespass in the 1930s must have thought that the legal right to walk in open country would be won after the Second World War, at the time when the National Parks were being created and the rights-of-way network drawn up. It was not to be. It was another half century before, finally, Parliament passed the Countryside and Rights of Way Act 2000, and the people of England and Wales gained the legal right to take to the hills and the moors. (Scotland has its own traditions and its own legislation.)

We have dedicated this series to the memory of Benny Rothman, one of the leaders of the 1932 Kinder Scout mass trespass who was imprisoned for his part in what was deemed a 'riotous assembly'. Later in his life, Benny Rothman was a familiar figure at rallies called by the Ramblers' Association as once again the issue of access rights came to the fore. But we should pay tribute to all who have campaigned for this goal. Securing greater access to the countryside was one of the principles on which the Ramblers' Association was founded in 1935, and for many ramblers the access legislation represents the achievement of literally a lifetime of campaigning.

So now, at last, we do have freedom to roam. For the first time in several centuries, the open mountains, moors and heaths of England and Wales are legally open for all. We have the protected right to get our boots wet in the peat bogs, to flounder in the tussocks, to blunder and scrabble through the bracken and heather, and to discover countryside which, legally, we had no way of knowing before.

The Freedom to Roam series of books has one aim: to encourage you to explore and grow to love these new areas of the countryside which are now open to us. The right to roam freely – that's surely something to celebrate.

Andrew Bibby
Series editor

Walking in open country –
a guide to using this book

If the right and the freedom to roam openly are so important – perceptive readers may be asking – why produce a set of books to tell you where to go?

So a word of explanation about this series. The aim is certainly not to encourage walkers to follow each other ant-like over the hills, sticking rigidly to a pre-determined itinerary. We are not trying to be prescriptive, instructing you on your walk stile by stile or gate by gate. The books are not meant as instruction manuals but we hope that they will be valuable as *guides* – helping you discover areas of the countryside which you haven't legally walked on before, advising you on routes you might want to take and telling you about places of interest on the way.

In areas where it can be tricky to find routes or track down landmarks, we offer more detailed instructions.

Elsewhere, we are deliberately less precise in our directions, allowing you to choose your own path or line to follow. For each walk, however, there is a recommended core route, and this forms the basis on which the distances given are calculated.

There is, then, an assumption that those who use this book will be comfortable with using a map – and that, in practice, means one of the Ordnance Survey's 1:25 000 Explorer series of maps. As well as referring to the maps in this book, it is worth taking the full OS map with you, to give you a wider picture of the countryside you will be exploring.

Safety in the hills

Those who are already experienced upland walkers will not be surprised if at this point we put in a note on basic safety in the hills. Walkers do need to remember that walking in open country, particularly high country, is different from footpath walking across farmland or more gentle countryside. The main risk is of being inadequately prepared for changes in the weather. Even in high summer, hail and even snow are not impossible. Daniel Defoe found this out in August 1724 when he crossed the Pennines from Rochdale, leaving a calm clear day behind to find himself almost lost in a blizzard on the tops.

If rain comes, the temperature will drop, so it is important when taking to the hills to be properly equipped and to guard against the risk of hypothermia. Fortunately, walkers today have access to a range of wind- and rain-proof clothing which was not available in the eighteenth century. Conversely, in hot weather, take sufficient water to avoid dehydration and hyperthermia (dangerous overheating of the body).

Be prepared for visibility to drop, when (to use the local term) the clag descends on the hills. It is always sensible to take a compass. If you are unfamiliar with basic compass-and-map work, ask in a local outdoor equipment shop whether they have simple guides available or pick the brains of a more experienced walker.

The other main hazard, even for walkers who know the hills well, is that of suffering an accident such as a broken limb. If you plan to walk alone, it is sensible to let someone know in advance where you will be walking and when you expect to be back – the moorland and mountain rescue services which operate in the areas covered by this book are very experienced but they are not psychic. Groups of walkers should tackle only what the least experienced or least fit member of the party can comfortably achieve. Take particular care if you intend to take children with you to hill country. And take a mobile phone by all means, but don't assume you can rely on it in an emergency, since some parts of the moors and hills will not pick up a signal. (If you can make a call and are in a real emergency situation, ring 999 – it is the police who coordinate mountain and moorland rescues.)

If this all sounds off-putting, that is certainly not the intention. The guiding principle behind the access legislation is that walkers will exercise their new-won rights with responsibility. Taking appropriate safety precautions is simply one aspect of acting responsibly.

Access land – what you can and can't do

The countryside which is covered by access legislation includes mountain, moor, heath, downland and common land. After the passing of the Countryside and Rights of Way Act 2000, a lengthy mapping process was undertaken, culminating in the production of 'conclusive' maps which identify land that is open for access. These maps (although not intended as guides for walking) can be accessed via the Internet, at www.countrysideaccess.gov.uk. Ordnance Survey maps

Note: Each walk has been graded, on a scale of
🥾 to 🥾 🥾 🥾 🥾 🥾 ,
for the degree of difficulty involved. In general, walks are judged more difficult if they are (a) longer in mileage, and/or (b) involve more rough walking (across open moorland rather than on established footpaths), and/or (c) pose more navigational problems or venture into very unfrequented areas. But bear in mind that all the walks in this book require map-reading competence and some experience of hill walking.

published from 2004 onwards also show the access land.

You can walk, run, birdwatch and climb on access land, although there is no new right to camp or to bathe in streams or lakes (or, of course, to drive vehicles). Dogs can come too, but the regulations sensibly insist that they are kept on leads near livestock and during the bird-nesting season (1 March to 31 July). Some grouse moors can ban dogs altogether, so you will need to watch out for local signs. Access legislation also does not include the right to ride horses or bikes, though in some areas there may be pre-existing agreements which allow this. More information is available on the website given above and, at the time

of writing, there is an advice line on 0845 100 3298.

The access legislation allows for some open country to be permanently excluded from the right to roam. 'Excepted' land includes military land, quarries and areas close to buildings; in addition landowners can apply for other open land to be excluded. For example, at the time of writing, a number of small areas of moorland which are used as rifle ranges have been designated in this way (these are not, however, in areas covered by walks in this book).

To the best of the authors' knowledge, all the walks in the Freedom to Roam series are either on legal rights of way or across access land included in the official 'conclusive' maps. However,

Nelson's Three Ships, Birchin Edge

you are asked to bear in mind that the books have been produced right at the beginning of the new access arrangements, before walkers have begun regularly to walk the hills and before any teething problems on the ground have been ironed out. For instance, at the time of writing there were still some places where entry arrangements to access land had not been finalized. As access becomes better established, it may be that minor changes to the routes suggested in these books will become appropriate or necessary. You are asked to remember that we are encouraging you to be flexible in the way you use these guides.

Walkers in open country also need to be aware that landowners have a further right to suspend or restrict access on their land for up to twenty-eight days a year. (In such cases of temporary closure there will normally still be access on public holidays and on most weekends.) Notice of closure needs to be given in advance, and the plan is that this information should be readily available to walkers, it is hoped at local information centres and libraries but also on the countryside access website and at popular entry points to access land. This sort of set-up has generally worked well in Scotland, where arrangements have been put in place to make sure that walkers in areas where deer hunting takes place can find out when and where hunting is happening.

Walkers will understand the sense in briefly closing small areas of open countryside when, for example, shooting is in progress (grouse shooting begins on 12 August) or when heather burning is taking place in spring. However, it is once again too early in the implementation of the access legislation to know how easily walkers in England and Wales will be able to find out about these temporary access closures. It is also too early to know whether landowners will attempt to abuse this power.

In some circumstances additional restrictions on access can be introduced – for example, on the grounds of nature conservation or heritage conservation, on the advice of English Nature and English Heritage.

Bear these points in mind, but enjoy your walking in the knowledge that any access restrictions should be the exception and not the norm. The Countryside Agency has itself stated that 'restrictions will be kept to a minimum'. If you do find access unexpectedly denied while walking in the areas suggested in this book, please accept the restrictions and follow the advice you are given. However, if you feel that access was wrongly denied, please report your experience to the countryside service of the local authority (or National Park authority, in National Park areas), and to the Ramblers' Association.

Finally, there may be occasions when you choose voluntarily not to exercise your freedom to roam. For example, many of the upland moors featured in these books are the homes of ground-nesting birds such as grouse, curlew, lapwing and pipit, who will be building their nests in spring and early summer. During this time, many people will decide to leave the birds in peace and find other places to walk. Rest assured that you will know if you are approaching an important nesting area – birds are good at telling you that they would like you to go away.

Celebrating the open countryside

Despite these necessary caveats, the message from this series is, we hope, clear. Make the most of the new legal rights we have been given – and enjoy your walking.

Andrew Bibby

Introduction

John Jordan – known as Jack – was one of the fourteen men and women who answered the clarion call from G.H.B. Ward, a twenty-two-year-old engineering fitter from Sheffield, to join him on a ramble around Kinder Scout on Sunday 2 September 1900 – the day which was to see the formation of the legendary Sheffield Clarion Ramblers' Club.

Fifty-eight years later, soon after Bert Ward's death, Jack Jordan concluded his account of that momentous day in the *Clarion Handbook* of 1958/9 with a strangely prophetic poem which encapsulates the spirit and ideals of those early Clarion Ramblers, and of all those who fought for the right to roam:

> *On a far-off autumn evening*
> *In the rays of the setting sun*
> *We sat and talked of Kinder*
> *And planned for the days to come.*
>
> *Bert was a man with a vision*
> *His thoughts on the hills afar*
> *As we pledged ourselves to the Clarion*
> *And hitched our faith to a star.*
>
> *There were those who called us dreamers*
> *But dreams can all come true*
> *If you have faith and work for them*
> *And ignore the scorn of the few.*
>
> *Today you roam o'er Kinder*
> *On paths that are yours by right*
> *But don't forget in your roaming*
> *For those paths WE had to fight.*

Yes, Kinder and many another
That today you regard as your own
Were keepered and labelled 'Private'
Till the Clarion came to roam!

So as you plan for the future
And the way seems bright and clear
Remember the flag-unfurlers
And all that we held most dear!

The Peak District's eastern moors, forbidden though many of them were to the public, were the playground of Bert Ward – the so-called King of the Clarion Ramblers – and many other climbers and ramblers from the grim back streets, who worked in the forges and cutlers' shops of the steel city of Sheffield. They were fortunate, as today's Sheffielders are, to have such a marvellous expanse of heather-clad moorland and inviting crags right on their doorsteps, but in those bad old days much of it was barred to walkers and strictly marshalled by belligerent gamekeepers.

In 1934 Phil Barnes, another famous Sheffield rambler and campaigner for access, published *Trespassers will be Prosecuted*, a beautifully photographed portfolio of 'Views of the Forbidden Moorlands of the Peak District'. In it he included a map of the roads and footpaths between Sheffield and Manchester, which showed an enormous blank covering 215 square miles (557 sq km) of moorland. Thirty-seven square miles (ninety-six square kilometres) of Bleaklow's open country were uncrossed by public paths. On Kinder, it was fifteen square miles (forty square kilometres). The moors to the east of the River Derwent, including Broomhead, Howden and Derwent moors, stretched for thirty-two square miles (eighty-three square kilometres) and had only three undisputed rights of way across them.

Most of these areas were privately owned grouse moors. But what angered Barnes more than anything else was the vast expanse of publicly owned land which was barred to the people, mainly in the interests of purity of reservoir water. He said there was a total of about 39,000 such acres, of which 28,000 was moorland.

'Surely in these publicly owned moors free access should be the rule and an example set to the private landowner,' claimed Barnes. 'The latter can hardly be expected to grant the concession refused by the public authority.' He added: 'If public access to the moors stretching for miles *beyond* the reservoirs can be seriously considered as a threat to public health, then surely there is no excuse for allowing the public to use the highways and footpaths which in many cases lie along the banks of reservoirs or adjoin streams running into them . . . But let us be impartial in such a matter and debar the sportsmen with their dogs as well as the farmers and their sheep; the gamekeepers as well as the ramblers!

'When the moors which could so fittingly be the playground of the people are thus rendered desolate, the water will be surprisingly pure and public health will only have those microbes to contend with, which have had the manners to remain where they were bred – in the crowded slums of the towns.'

And Barnes quoted from the *Manchester Guardian*, a long-time supporter of the access cause, from 21 April 1925: 'There is something wantonly perverse and profane in a society in which the rights of property can be used to defeat the emotions in which mankind has found its chief inspiration and comfort. If ever any truth lurked in the phrase "the rights

Ramblers on Kinder in 1906

of man", those rights should surely include the right to climb mountains and the right to dream beside the sea.'

Now at last most of these publicly owned moors are again open country for all to enjoy. Many of the walks in this book explore their scenic beauty as well as the rich legacy of enigmatic remains left behind by their prehistoric settlers.

While the main focus in this book (and in its companion volume about the northern and western Peak District) is on the Dark Peak moors, some walks from further south have nevertheless been included. Many previously private limestone dalesides are now open, and interesting newly accessible areas, including Eldon and Ecton Hills and the reef limestone hills of the upper Dove, are covered in this guide.

The Peak District stands at the crossroads of Britain. It is the place where many southern lowland species, such as the ivy-leaved bell flower, the stemless thistle and the nuthatch, are at their northern limit and where many northern upland species, such as the cowberry and bearberry, the globe flower, the melancholy thistle and the mountain hare, reach their southernmost extension. This, together with the wide variety of geological and landscape types within the area, makes it a paradise for the naturalist, who can see a great variety of wildlife and plant life in a very small area.

The limestone White Peak, which occupies the central and southern areas of the National Park, has a gentle, almost feminine quality. Lushly vegetated, steep-sided dales, rich with wildflowers in the summer and watered by crystal-clear streams like the Dove (Walk 12) and the Manifold (Walk 11), dissect the broad limestone plateau, where miles of dry-stone walls criss-cross emerald meadows like a net holding down the billowing landscape.

The limestone dales are by far the richest wildlife habitats in the Peak and over fifty species of wildflowers and herbs are typically found in each square metre (ten square feet) of their lime-rich grasslands. The species include the rare and lovely pink-flowered shrub mezereon, which is found in the ash woodland of Dovedale.

Dovedale's ash woods are nationally important, although surprisingly this most famous of all the limestone dales is not part of the Derbyshire Dales National Nature Reserve. Most of the dale, with striking reef limestone crags especially in its upper reaches (Walk 12), is however in the safe hands of the National Trust. The Derbyshire and Staffordshire wildlife trusts also have important reserves in the Wye and Manifold valleys.

Most of the common British mammals can be found in the limestone dales, including the otter which has recently made a welcome reappearance. Birdlife includes the dipper and grey wagtail, ubiquitous in and around the rivers.

In direct counterpoint to the White Peak, and enclosing it to the north, east and west in an upturned horseshoe, is the more masculine gritstone Dark Peak. The base rock here is millstone grit, a coarse, abrasive sandstone which outcrops in the famous east Peakland 'edges' – short but steep escarpments like Derwent Edge (Walk 4) and Bamford and Stanage Edges (Walk 5), which look down on the valley of the Derwent.

The Dark Peak supports a much less varied wildlife than the White. In the rocky cloughs (steep-sided valleys) of the moorland streams, the clear song of the ring ouzel can often be heard, while golden plover and curlew are the most common waders seen or heard on the moor tops. And in winter an increasingly common sight, especially on the eastern moors, is the conspicuous white coat of the mountain hare, which was re-introduced to the area during the nineteenth century for sporting purposes (see pages 33–4).

There are also the moorland birds of prey, particularly the peregrine falcon, the merlin, the goshawk and the hen harrier, all of which are enjoying something of a revival after many years of persecution. That persecution came mainly from those same gamekeepers who tried to keep ramblers off the moors. However, it should be remembered that we owe the tapestry of purple heather, which is one of the joys of a moorland walk in late summer, to those gamekeepers who manage these moors almost exclusively for the red grouse.

The limestone of the White Peak is the bare bones of the landscape and the oldest rock exposed in the area. Laid down under a shallow tropical sea during the Carboniferous period about 350 million years ago, the limestone consists of the remains of millions upon millions of microscopic sea creatures who lived and died in that ancient sea at a time when what is now known as the Peak District was close to the Equator. You can still see the remains of these fossilized land-building skeletons in the stones of the dry-stone walls or in gateposts and the typical 'squeezer' stiles, where the screw-like stems of crinoids (sea lilies) have been polished by years of abrasion.

On the edges of this tropical lagoon, harder limestones built up in reefs, just as they are doing today in places like Australia's Great Barrier Reef. This harder reef limestone gives us the few real peaks in the area, like the mineral-rich Ecton Hill in the Manifold valley (Walk 11) and the isolated ridge peaks of Chrome, Parkhouse and High Wheeldon in the upper Dove (Walk 12). Later, meltwater from Ice Age glaciers gouged out the steep-sided limestone dales, and the slightly acidic rainwater took advantage of the bedding planes and cracks in the limestone to hollow out the caves of the White Peak, such as Thor's Cave in the Manifold valley. Some White Peak rivers, like the Manifold and the Hamps, disappear underground for much of their course during the summer months.

Later during the same geological epoch, the limestone was buried under coarse sediments, grits and mudbanks which spread out in great deltas from huge rivers flowing from the north. These darker sediments overlaid the limestone and after aeons of time were petrified into the shale, sandstone and gritstone of the Dark Peak, later to be pushed up into the 'Derbyshire Dome'.

Whereas the limestone was porous and dissolved in water, the gritstone of the Dark Peak was impervious and poorly drained. So any vegetation which grew on the surface, like sphagnum moss, bilberry and heather, quickly rotted down to form immense layers of peat, creating the bleak moorland landscapes of today.

The major rivers of the north and eastern Peak, such as the Derwent and Wye, exploited the shale valleys which form the border between the limestone and gritstone, and they now flow in broad valleys to join the Trent and eventually reach the North Sea.

The White Peak was the first area of the Peak to be permanently inhabited by humans following the retreat of the glaciers about 10,000 years ago. The earliest evidence of human activity in the area is the isolated 'microliths' – tiny flakes of flint – which are often found in the peat of the eastern moors (Walk 2), providing evidence of the hunting activities of mesolithic (middle Stone Age) man about 8,500 years ago.

Remains of neolithic (later Stone Age) man have been found in rock shelters and caves in many White Peak dales, including Dowel Dale (Walk 12), and possibly at Carl Wark (Walk 6) and on Gardom's Edge (Walk 8). But the most thoroughly investigated of the prehistoric remains in the Peak are the moorlands of the Dark Peak flanking the eastern side of the Derwent, where entire Bronze Age landscapes, from field systems to burial monuments, were found to lie fossilized under the heather and bracken. One example is Swine Sty on Big Moor (Walk 7). A rare example of Bronze Age cup-and-ring 'rock art' can also be seen between Gardom's and Birchen Edge (Walk 8).

Archaeologists believe that this area, which is now almost all moorgrass and heather, may have been over-farmed in this period. As a consequence, and also as a result of a deterioration in the climate, human occupation tended to shift in succeeding generations further south to the White Peak region.

After the Norman Conquest, much of the northern part of the Peak District became a forty-square-mile (hundred-square-kilometre) royal forest, reserved for hunting (Walk 10). The forest was administered from William Peveril's castle above Castleton, and the Forest Chamber, where the officials meted out punishments for offenders against the strict forest law, was at Peak Forest.

The great age of rebuilding, which took place in the seventeenth and eighteenth centuries, created the well-known mansions of Haddon, Eyam Hall, Lyme Park and the original Chatsworth, as important landowners sought to demonstrate their power and wealth. The formerly open landscape was gradually enclosed as these landowners took in more and more moorland for cultivation, creating the familiar pattern of stone-walled fields we see today.

Mineral wealth, especially from lead (which had brought the Romans to the Peak) and from copper was another major source of income for the landed gentry, and during the eighteenth and nineteenth centuries the lead and copper mining industries of the White Peak became very important. Even today, the limestone plateau is littered with the remains of the workings. The most famous lead mine is the Magpie mine near Sheldon, now run as a field-study centre; but in their heyday during the eighteenth century the Duke of Devonshire's copper mines at Ecton Hill in the Manifold valley were equally if not more profitable (Walk 11).

After the gradual spread across the Peakland moors of turnpike roads, often following old routes marked by guide stoops, the railways arrived. Among the last in the railway age was the short-lived Leek and Manifold Light Railway (Walk 11), which since 1937 has served as the Manifold Track walking and riding route.

At this time too came the reservoirs to provide drinking water for the new industrial cities, such as Manchester, Sheffield and Derby, which were springing up around the edges of the Peak. The most famous reservoirs are the three which flooded the upper section of the Derwent valley – the Howden, Derwent and Ladybower (Walk 4), and the five which filled the Longdendale valley in the north of the National Park (Walk 1).

Pressure from the populations of the industrial cities and towns for better access to the moorland countryside, which had been available to all before the enclosure movement, was one of the most important influences behind the creation of the Peak District National Park – the first in Britain – in April 1951. But the National Park is also there to conserve the last remaining green space in the south Pennines from unsuitable industrial and residential development, and to protect the area's wildlife.

Whether White Peak or Dark, the area covered by this book is a place to escape urban pressures and enjoy the countryside, with something for everybody. Joseph W. Batty, writing in the 1950/51 Jubilee Edition of the *Clarion Handbook*, was concerned that the efforts of the Clarion Ramblers would end up being taken for granted and that the achievements of Bert Ward would be forgotten in future years:

> *Will Ward gain thanks in all the years to be*
> *For all he did to help the poor roam free*
> *On moor and hill? It may be that he will,*
> *But more than likely that his name will pass*
> *Along the mem'ries of his printed page.*

Batty needn't have worried: the spirit of Bert Ward, the King of the Clarions, still strides these once forbidden moors.

WALK 1

SNAILSDEN MOOR AND RAMSDEN CLOUGH

DIFFICULTY 👢 👢 👢 👢 👢

DISTANCE About 10 miles (16 km)

SALTER'S BROOK BRIDGE		WITHINS EDGE		RAMSDEN CLOUGH		COOK'S STUDY HILL		SNAILSDEN PIKE END		SALTER'S BROOK BRIDGE
	DEAD EDGE END		BRITLAND EDGE HILL		SNAILSDEN RESERVOIR		SNAILSDEN RESERVOIR		DEAD EDGE END	

MAP OS Explorer OL1, The Peak District – Dark Peak area

STARTING POINT Salter's Brook Bridge on the A628
(GR 136001)

PARKING In car park at Salter's Brook Bridge

PUBLIC TRANSPORT Buses from Sheffield and Manchester

The 14 square miles (36 sq km) of Withens Moor and Snailsden Moor, north of Salter's Brook Bridge on the A628, were the last bastion of the forbidden sporting estates in the Peak, but are now finally in open access.

Containing the sources of the Mersey and the Don, these desolate moors demand both respect and stamina to cross them. This is a strenuous walk that should only be attempted in good weather. The route passes

over the Woodhead tunnels, which were among the longest anywhere in the British rail network.

▶ The walk starts at the car park by the side of Salter's Brook Bridge. This is on the A628 about a mile (1.6 km) east of the portals of the Woodhead railway tunnels, at the eastern end of Longdendale.

■ The Woodhead railway line was the first to cross the formidable barrier of the Pennines. It was built by the Sheffield, Aston-under-Lyme and Manchester Railway between 1837 and 1845 and involved the construction of the 3-mile (4.8-km) Woodhead Tunnel under the bleak Woodhead Moors, at a cost of £200,000. A total of 157 tons of gunpowder was used to make the tunnel, but it soon proved too small, and work started on a second, parallel tunnel in 1847. This construction was marred by tragedy, when in 1848 a cholera epidemic claimed the lives of twenty-eight navvies, most of whom are buried at St James' Church in Woodhead.

A third tunnel was built in 1949 to take the newly electrified line, but it lasted less than thirty years before final closure in the 1960s. One of the old bores was re-used to take the 400,000-volt power lines which thread Longdendale under the moors, obviating the need for unsightly pylons. The line of the railway through Longdendale is now followed by the Trans-Pennine Trail.

Salter's Brook Bridge, across the stream of the same name, recalls the old salters' route from Cheshire to Yorkshire through Longdendale. Near by are the ruins of the former Lady Cross shooting cabin, and the former Miller's Arms public house, which closed in 1917. The Miller's Arms was the venue for an annual shepherds' gathering in times gone by.

▶ Make your way up Salter's Brook across Longside Moss towards the prominent blockhouse ahead, which marks one of five shafts used initially to take out the overburden from the construction of the Woodhead tunnels, and used later for ventilation. Don't be alarmed if you see 'smoke' emerging from the shafts. It is not a ghost train but condensation rising from the coolant used on the underground power lines.

Passing the spoil tips from the tunnel excavations and heading north-east along Upper Head Dike towards the bowl of Red Hole you cross the line of the tunnels, about 150 ft (45 m) below this section of rough, tussock-grassed moorland.

■ The clear waters of Red Hole Spring on the side of Round Hill could claim to be the true source of the mighty Mersey. The water flows down into Salter's Brook and then the Etherow, now dammed by the five reservoirs which fill Longdendale, before flowing on to Liverpool and into the Irish Sea.

▶ The next objective in the virtually featureless moorland is the trig point (GR 124017) on Dead Edge End ❶ at 1637 ft (499 m). There are views across

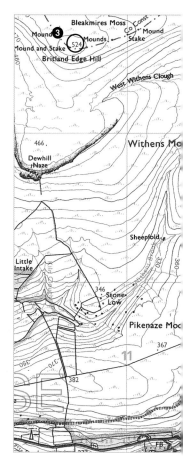

Dead Edge Flat down steep-sided Dearden Clough towards the waters of the Winscar reservoir above Dunford Bridge, where the Woodhead tunnels emerge.

■ Dearden Clough and Dearden Moss take their names from Henry James Dearden, a well-known Sheffield brewer and

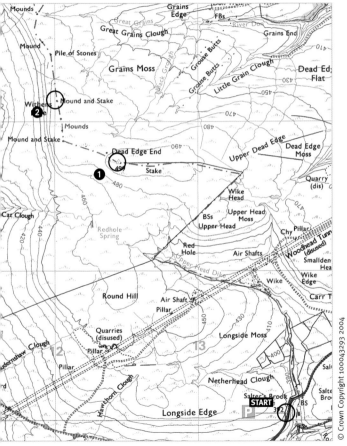

© Crown Copyright 100043293 2004

▶ Map continues northwards on pages 30–31

sportsman, and his son, Hardress Dearden. These sportsmen both regularly shot on these moors, and were instrumental in introducing the mountain or blue hare to the northern Peak District in the late nineteenth century (see pages 33–4).

Just below and to the north of Dead Edge End, the waters of Black Grough run down towards Winscar reservoir. This flows east across Grains Moss to form the infant River Don, which eventually flows through the city of Sheffield. Thus, less than a mile (1.6 km) apart and on one of the great watersheds of England, we pass the sources of the rivers which flow through two of the North's most important cities – Sheffield and Manchester.

▶ Following an intermittent line of boundary mounds and stakes, head north now along Withens Edge ❷, with Withens Moor and the valley of Withens Brook down to your left. Continue along this boundary line, which marks the division between Yorkshire and Derbyshire, as it turns west by a prominent mound to reach the summit of Britland Edge Hill – at 1719 ft (524 m) the highest point of the walk (GR 106026) ❸.

■ On a good day, there are glorious views from here. To the north, the thin needle of the Holme Moss television mast threads the clouds and dominates the *Last of the Summer Wine* country around

Holmfirth. To the west are the wilds of Black Hill and the Saddleworth Moors, with Bleaklow visible to the south and the Langsett Moors to the east.

▶ Retrace your steps to the mound where the route turned west and follow the stream which runs north-east down from the aptly named Bleakmires Moss towards the beautiful little valley of Ramsden Clough ❹.

■ This is one of the secret and until now unseen gems of the Dark Peak, rivalling the ravine of Kinder Downfall in its wild beauty. A rocky amphitheatre – including Ramsden Rocks and the Rakes below Herbage Hill on the western bank, and the crags on Lad Clough Knoll on the east – forms the narrow, V-shaped head of the clough. It is certainly worth a careful exploration of its

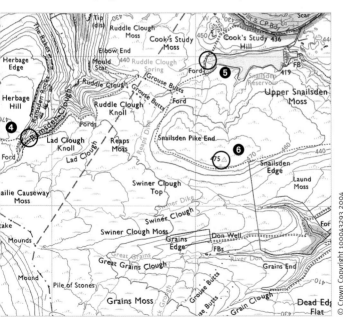

© Crown Copyright 100043293 2004

steep, boulder-filled depths. Unfortunately, at the time of writing, access has not been agreed to the lower, northern entrance to the clough via Holme and the plantations of Riding Wood reservoir.

▶ Retracing your steps out of Ramsden Clough, you have a choice of routes. You could go south back to Withens Edge and Dead End Edge, to return to Salter's Brook via Upper Head Dike. The ankle-testing alternative is to head east across Ruddle Clough Knoll and Cook's Study Moss and descend by a track which takes you round to the road at the western end of Snailsden reservoir ❺.

Turn right at the road and right again to cross under the reservoir embankment to Upper Snailsden Moss. Climb the rough moorland to the trig point (GR 132033) on Snailsden End Pike (1558 ft/475 m) ❻, another fine viewpoint north across the Holme valley towards Holmfirth.

Now you are faced with 2 miles (3.2 km) more of very strenuous bog-trotting, heading south and crossing the streams of Swiner Clough and the infant Don below Great Grains Clough and Black Clough. Eventually a line of grouse butts can be followed heading south-west towards Dead Edge End and your outward route back to Salter's Brook Bridge.

A shepherds' gathering at the former Miller's Arms pub, Longdendale

Hare today, gone tomorrow

The mountain or blue hare (*Lepus timidis*) is often the highlight of a walk across the eastern and northern moors of the Peak District. After sitting quite still in its form (a depression in the ground) among the boulders and tors of the Dark Peak, at the approach of a walker it will suddenly burst from cover and dash across the peat haggs (banks) and groughs (channels).

It is the hare's unfortunate habit of changing the colour of its coat from the dull greyish brown of summer to a bluish grey in autumn and finally pure white in winter which makes it so obvious. The hare has not yet adapted to the milder, often snow-free winters of today, and the clever camouflage device now has exactly the opposite effect – making the hares much more conspicuous against the dark background of peat and heather.

The story of the Peak's population of mountain hares is an interesting one. Introduced to the area by the Dearden family of Sheffield in the late nineteenth century, the hares were originally natives of Scotland, where their ability to change colour to white in the snowy Highland winters gave them valuable protection against their natural predators: golden eagles, wildcats and foxes.

The reason for their introduction to the Peak District was to provide extra sporting interest for the growing numbers of marksmen of the late Victorian age. The population of mountain hares has fluctuated in more recent years after the shooting interest waned, but generally they have thrived on the higher eastern and northern moors of the Peak District and are at their southernmost limit in Britain here.

Their greatest threat today is the climate, and cold, wet springs can lead to high mortality among the leverets, which are born around this time. Many hares are also killed on the higher roads which cross the Peak, such as the A57 trans-Pennine Snake Pass.

Another rarity at its southern limit on the north-eastern moors of the Peak District is an aromatic bushy shrub called Labrador tea (*Ledum groenlandicum*). A native of North America and Greenland, this creamy white-flowered shrub looks like a dwarf azalea, with thick, leathery dark green leaves designed to help reduce transpiration in an exposed environment. How Labrador tea reached the moors of the Peak District is still a mystery, but among the theories is the rather unlikely one that seeds were blown across the Atlantic or carried by migrating birds. Another possibility is that they represent the relict population of an ancient plant migration.

WALK 2

LANGSETT MOORS

DIFFICULTY 🥾 🥾 🥾 🥾   **DISTANCE 6 miles (9.6 km)**

| LANGSETT BARN | NORTH AMERICA | MICKLEDEN EDGE | CUT GATE | LOST LAD | PIKE LOWE | UPPER MIDHOPE | LANGSETT BARN |

MAP OS Explorer OL1, The Peak District – Dark Peak area

STARTING POINT Langsett Barn car park on the A616 Stocksbridge–Flouch road (GR 210004)

PARKING In the car park

PUBLIC TRANSPORT Buses from Sheffield and Stocksbridge

While the moors to the west of Langsett have been subject to access agreements for some time, the Midhope Moors have long been out of bounds to walkers. The new access legislation has thus opened up a largely unknown area of the National Park, which features the prehistoric burial cairn of Pike Lowe and the remains of much wartime training activity.

■ Langsett Barn, a magnificent, cathedral-like structure dating from the seventeenth century, was converted to an information centre, ranger base and community centre for the village of Langsett in 1993. Although the information

centre no longer exists, the project was an excellent example of co-operation between local authorities, in this case the Peak District National Park, Barnsley Metropolitan Council and Yorkshire Water.

The village of Langsett gets its name from the Old English for 'long slope', which describes perfectly the situation of the village where the Midhope Moors run down to the Porter, or Little Don, river. This is, incidentally, one of very few rivers in Britain with two official names on the OS map.

▶ Leave the car park by the gate which leads down through Langsett Bank Woods to a path heading right, through the trees alongside the Langsett reservoir. The path rises to the stone-built Brookhouse Bridge which spans the Porter or Little Don, where it joins the ancient bridleway known as the Cut Gate track and goes down to cross the bridge.

■ The Cut (or Cart) Gate is an ancient track which was used

by farmers in the upper Derwent and Woodlands valley to take their livestock to Penistone Market. The track runs from the reconstructed Slippery Stones Bridge at the head of the Howden reservoir up Bull Clough and over Featherbed Moss to Mickleden Edge, before dropping over Hingcliff Hill and into Langsett.

Near the bridge are the remains of Brookhouse Farm, which was one of several which were demolished in the interests of water purity when the reservoir was built. According to a local legend, in 1588 the rent for this farm was said to be a red rose at Christmas and a snowball at midsummer.

▶ Go through the gate and up the hillside opposite on a track which soon leaves the trees behind and enters open moorland at Delf Edge. The way now climbs steadily over Hingcliff Common towards Hingcliff Hill. Where the path forks, take the left-hand alternative which leads down, with views across the

reservoir and its encircling trees, towards the forlorn ruins of an old farmstead known as North America (GR 203997) ❶.

■ During the 'Age of Discovery' in the eighteenth and nineteenth centuries, it was customary to name isolated farms after the places which were, in those days, on the edge of the known world. So farms with names like North America, Quebec and Botany Bay are quite common in the Midland counties. North America Farm, like Brookhouse passed earlier, was abandoned when the reservoir was built.

The pockmarks in some of the stones of the broken-down walls were caused when the ruined farm was used in the Second World War for target practice by troops in training for the D-Day landings, some of whom were stationed near Langsett. Take care, for it is not uncommon to find live ammunition in the heather in these parts. There will be further evidence of the former military presence later on in the walk.

▶ The route now ascends directly behind the ruined farm, heading in a south-westerly direction to the right of the wall which runs up Stanny Common.

■ Beautifully crafted barbed and tongued prehistoric flint arrowheads have been found in the peat close to this track and also near to Cut Gate, showing that these moors were used by hunter-gathers as far back as the Bronze Age. The climate was warmer in those days, but it is thought that these early settlers would only have ventured here in the summer season.

▶ After about a mile (1.6 km) of walking and almost opposite Bradshaw Hill the track, now a faint and peaty path, reaches the deep ravine of Mickleden Edge ❷, with scattered trees alongside the banks of Mickleden Brook below. Here the path is joined by the Cut Gate track, which has come up directly from Hingcliff Hill on the right. The route now follows Cut Gate and the edge in a southerly direction.

Where the ridge peters out and the path comes to the head of Mickleden Brook, the slight ridge known as Lost Lad ❸ appears on the left.

■ It is possible that Lost Lad gained its name in a similar way to the identically named height below Back Tor on Derwent Edge, recalling the sad tale of a young shepherd boy who became lost on the moors in the winter snows and whose body was eventually found near the spot named after him.

A more prosaic explanation is that 'lad' can also be used in the north of England to mean a guide stone.

▶ Leave the path and head left across the open moor towards the map spot height of 479 m at Sugden Top (GR 196975). Follow the broad top of Candlerush Edge – which probably gets its name from the soft rushes found here, which were used to make wicks for candles in years gone by –

towards the encircling boulder field and beckoning cairn on the summit of Pike Lowe (GR 209973) **❹**, just 3 ft (90 cm) lower than Sugden Top at 1568 ft (478 m).

■ Pike Lowe is a large prehistoric burial mound of indeterminate age. Like its southern counterpart with the same name overlooking the Derwent dam on the eastern side of the upper Derwent valley, it most probably dates from the Bronze Age.

The views from the large cairn are extensive, looking east across to industrial Stocksbridge in the Don valley, with the tower blocks of Sheffield further south. The plumes of steam issuing from the Drax and Ferrybridge power stations on the River Ouse are also usually visible, along with the thirteen white propellers of the Royd Moor wind farm.

▶ Now head due north through the boulder field which surrounds Pike Lowe and descend gradually across the well-named Fenny Common – it is usually very wet –

until you reach the fences, walls and tank tracks which mark the remnants of the training area used by the Army during the Second World War. This area has been given the appropriate name of Range Moor.

Continue north until you reach the track which leads towards Thickwoods Lane by Thickwoods Plantation, ahead to the left.

■ Thickwoods Lane was reinforced to make it suitable for tanks during the Second World War. The red-brick rubble from which the track is made apparently came from bombed-out houses in nearby Sheffield.

▶ Through another gate, you reach a concrete track across which is a metal barrier. Go through the gap in the wall and turn left up a walled green lane which leads to the hamlet of Townend, the western end of the village of Upper Midhope ❺.

■ The twin villages of Upper Midhope and Midhopestones are of very ancient origin. Hope comes from an Old

Langsett reservoir

English word meaning 'a small, enclosed valley', which is a good description of the area. The tiny church of St James at Midhopestones was restored in 1705, and has a fine, much earlier Renaissance pulpit.

Across the valley of the Porter/Little Don from Upper Midhope, around Alderman's Head Farm, is the site of the lost market town of Penisale. It was granted the right to hold a market around an ancient oak tree in 1290, but nothing now remains.

▶ Turn left and then right through Townend and take the bridleway down to meet Joseph Lane until it joins the road. Turn left at the road to the pavement which crosses the embankment wall of the Langsett reservoir ❻.

■ The embankment of Langsett reservoir is 1156 ft (352 m) long and has a depth of 117 ft (35 m) to the former riverbed beneath. The reservoir itself holds over 1400 million gallons of water. The castellated valvehouse at the northern end of the dam wall is supposed to have been modelled on the gatehouse of Lancaster Castle. The dam took fourteen years to build, between 1889 and 1904, and the reservoir is now managed by Yorkshire Water. The naturally acidic, peaty-brown water is treated at Langsett Treatment Works just below the embankment wall to the right, which is on the site of the temporary village of corrugated iron huts where the navvies who built the dam lived. As at Birchinlee in the upper Derwent valley, their far from primitive facilities included a hospital, a canteen and recreation rooms.

▶ On reaching the junction with the A616 opposite the Bank View café, turn left and left again along a lane which leads past a large barn on your right. Turn left between two walls to return to the Langsett Barn car park.

WALK 3

BROOMHEAD AND BRADFIELD MOORS

DIFFICULTY 🥾 🥾 🥾 🥾 🥾   **DISTANCE 8 miles (13 km)**

| MORTIMER ROAD | | BROOMHEAD MOOR | | FLINT HILL | | EMLIN DIKE | | AGDEN BRIDGE | | MORTIMER ROAD |
| EWDEN BECK | | DUKE'S ROAD | | NEW CROSS | | BRADFIELD MOORS | | BAR DYKE |

MAP OS Explorer OL1, The Peak District – Dark Peak area

STARTING POINT Mortimer Road, near Broomhead Hall (GR 242962)

PARKING Limited parking available at starting point

PUBLIC TRANSPORT No buses closer than Stocksbridge

This is a very tough, 8- or 9-mile (13- or 14.5-km) excursion across mainly trackless moorland, all of which is on new access land. It crosses the deep heather of Broomhead and Bradfield Moors, which are rich in prehistoric remains, ancient trackways and landmarks.

▶ The walk starts from the point where the public footpath leaves the Mortimer or Strines Road opposite the forested grounds of Broomhead Hall, the former home of the Rimington Wilson family.

■ The original Broomhead Hall, overlooking the valley of the Ewden Beck, was built in the fourteenth century, and a second, the home of the staunch Parliamentarian

▶ page 46

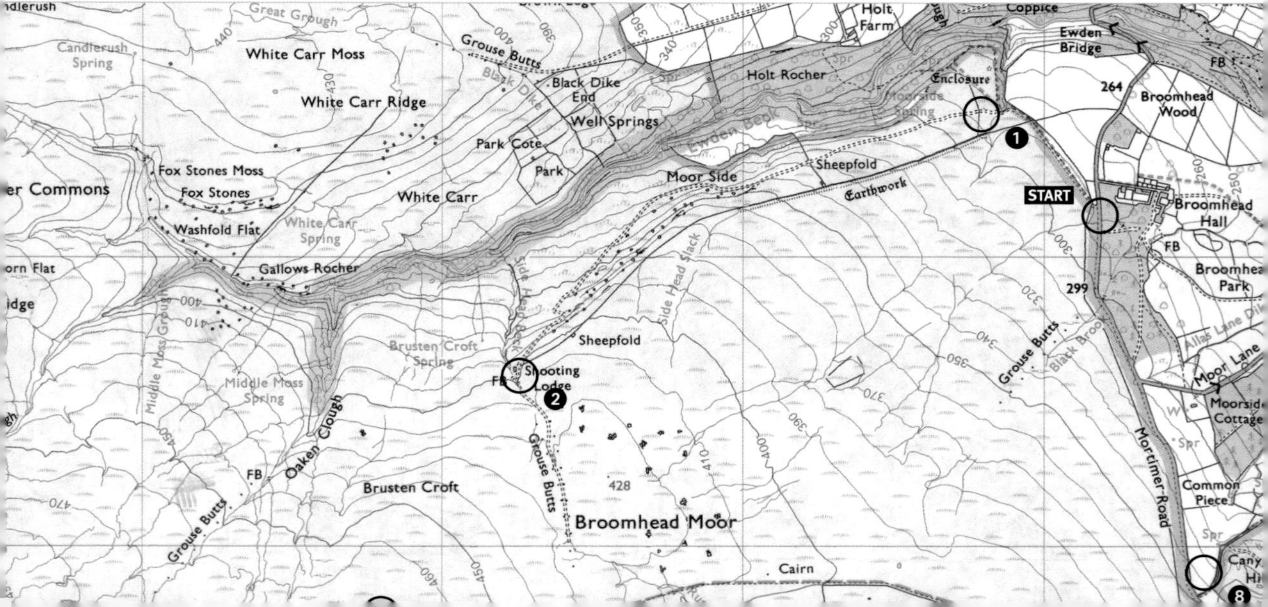
START
White Carr Moss
White Carr Ridge
Great Grough
Candlerush Spring
Grouse Butts
Black Dike
Black Dike End
Well Springs
Park Cote
Park
Fox Stones Moss
Fox Stones
Washfold Flat
White Carr
White Carr Spring
Gallows Rocher
Holt Rocher
Holt Farm
Coppice
Ewden Bridge
Ewden Beck
Enclosure
Moorside Spring
Broomhead Wood
Broomhead Hall
Broomhead Park
FB
Sheepfold
Moor Side
Earthwork
Side Head Slack
Side Head Beck
Shooting Lodge
Brusten Croft Spring
Brusten Croft
Middle Moss Spring
Middle Moss Grough
Oaken Clough
Broomhead Moor
Cairn
Black Brook
Allas Lane Dike
Moor Lane
Moorside Cottage
Common Piece
Mortimer Road
Spr
264
299
428

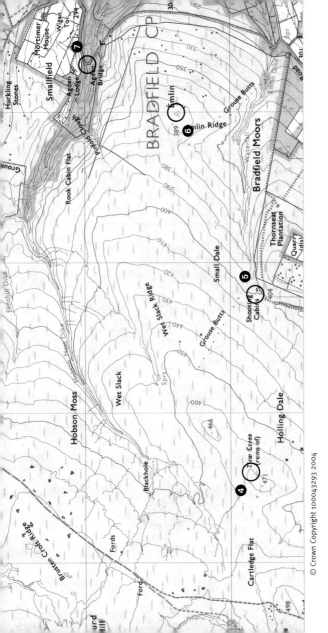

© Crown Copyright 100043293 2004

Christopher Wilson, took its place in 1640. The last building, now demolished, was erected by the (Rimington) Wilson family in 1831, and remained empty and derelict for many years. The oak table which used to stand in the hall was dated 1588 and was said to have been made from timbers from a wreck of the ill-fated Spanish Armada.

Mortimer Road, also known as the Strines Road, was a turnpike road constructed by an Act of Parliament of 1771, following the line of an ancient packhorse route known as Halifax Gate which linked Penistone with the Hope valley. It was built at the instigation of Hans Winthrop Mortimer, Lord of the Manor of Bamford, and completed around 1777. While it was never a commercial success, it remains one of the most scenic roads in the Peak District.

▶ Keep to the left of the enclosure wall on the path which leads through the deep heather

to a linear earthwork running in a roughly east–west direction for about ½ mile (0.8 km) along the southern edge of the Ewden Beck ❶.

■ This earthwork is obviously of ancient origin and probably a boundary ditch, but this has never been conclusively proved nor has it been dated. Near by is an area of many cairns and enclosures which date back to prehistoric times, including a 'stone circle', which may well be a hut circle. It was unknown to archaeologists until revealed after a moorland fire.

You are now looking down on the delightful wooded valley of the Ewden Beck. The word 'beck' comes from the Old Norse *bekkr* meaning a stream or brook. It is unusual in the Peak District, being more often found further north in the Yorkshire Dales and the Lake District. Opposite are the buildings of Holt Farm and the rocks of Holt Rocher, seen above the trees.

▶ Follow the track to the left (west) which runs north of the earthwork for about a mile (1.6 km) until you reach the shooting cabin which stands above the valley of Side Head Beck ❷. You now follow a line of grouse butts, still on the track, to the left (south) through the deepening heather up and across Broomhead Moor.

■ Broomhead Moor has the dubious distinction of being the place where a record grouse bag (an astonishing 1421½ brace, or 2843 birds) was shot in one August day in 1913.

▶ Where the track ends, follow the line of the infant Rushy Dike which will bring you down to the public bridleway known as the Duke's Road.

■ The Duke in question was the Duke of Norfolk, Lord of the Manor of Sheffield, who had extensive shooting interests in the area and the road was constructed for the use of his grouse-shooting guests. It was also the scene of a second, almost forgotten mass trespass in 1932, which took place five months after the better-known Kinder Scout trespass (see pages 52–3). G.H.B. Ward described this as 'the wildest Yorkshire moorland walk south of Wharfedale'.

▶ Turn right and follow the obvious bridleway as it gradually ascends Flint Hill (1545 ft/471 m) ❸. This may seem an odd name until you realize just how many prehistoric flint implements dating back to neolithic times have been found in the eroding peat of this area of Broomhead Moor. They were made from raw material from as far away as the Yorkshire Wolds – the nearest source of flint – and are still being found to this day.

To shorten the walk, about ½ mile (0.8 km) after joining the Duke's Road you could head off due south on a compass bearing for the shooting cabin on Broomhead Moor (GR 228928), but it is very rough going and you would have to cross the marshy ground of Hobson Moss Dyke.

The main route continues on the Duke's Road, heading south-west now along Brusten Croft Ridge to the rocks of Cartledge Flat (GR 207926) at 1634 ft (498 m), which overlook the deep trench of Abbey Brook. Leave Cartledge Flat in an easterly direction, crossing the boggy upper reaches of Hobson Moss Dyke and heading for New Cross (GR 218928) ❹.

■ One thing we can be certain of is that, despite its name, New Cross is anything but new. The lettering with which it is named on the OS map indicates its antiquity, and if this is the new cross we can assume that it replaced an even older one. It stands about midway along a hollow way (an ancient track hollowed out by centuries of use) which crossed the Bradfield Moors between Bradfield and Abbey Brook in the Derwent valley.

Research by G.H.B. Ward published in his *Clarion Handbook* of 1926 calls this route the Emlin Dike Road, and it was used as a shortcut by farmers from Bradfield who wanted to get to the Derwent valley. More recent research by Terry Howard of the Sheffield Campaign for Access to Moorland (SCAM) reveals that reference to a 40-ft (12-m) wide New Cross Road, crossing the moors from the Mortimer Road to Cartledge Flats, was made in the 1826 Enclosure Award.

All that remains of the once important landmark of New Cross is the weathered square gritstone base, which has a diagonally placed cross or sword carved on one side. The cross had a tapering shaft in Ward's day, but this is now missing. Terry Howard thinks the cross marked an old ecclesiastical boundary, perhaps showing the boundary of land owned by the Knights of St John or the Knights Templar.

▶ Leaving New Cross and its mysteries, head eastward across the wastes of Holling Dale towards the shooting cabin above a disused quarry near spot height 404 m on the map

(GR 228928) ❺. Here the footpath above Emlin Dike is followed along a line of old boundary marker stones on the former Emlin Dike Road. Follow the markers and a hollow way north-east and cross Emlin Dike above a little waterfall.

Ascend Emlin Ridge, following the old hollow ways through the bracken as they swing to the north of the trig point at 1276 ft (389 m) ❻ and down through the heather to the trees surrounding Agden Bridge ❼, back on the Mortimer Road. Turn left on to the road and ascend steeply past Mortimer House on the left to the top of the hill, where the enigmatic Dark Age earthwork known as the Bar Dike crosses the road, and the Duke's Road comes in from the left.

Shortly after passing the Bar Dyke and where the road comes up from Bradfield on the right, you pass the guide stoop known as Handsome or Hanson Cross ❽. It reads: 'Penniston 5m, Sheafeld 6m, Bradfield 1m 1753'.

■ Across the road the tumbled humps and hollows of the Canyards or Kanyars Hills are apparently an ancient landslip, which was once known as Mouldycliff. According to G.H.B. Ward this was a common name for such formations, like the similarly shaped Apple Pie Hill in Mickleden Clough.

▶ It is now less than a mile (1.6 km) along the Mortimer Road back to your starting point near Broomhead Hall.

The other trespass

Everybody in the rambling world has heard of the mass trespass which took place on Kinder Scout in April 1932, which served as an important catalyst both for the Freedom to Roam movement and the creation of the National Parks.

But there was also another, now largely forgotten mass trespass five months after the Kinder Scout event, when a group of about two hundred ramblers from Sheffield deliberately faced up to the landowners to exercise their cherished right to roam. The scene of this second trespass was the ancient highway known as the Duke of Norfolk's Road, which runs across Broomhead Moor to Abbey Brook in the upper Derwent valley.

Among the trespassers in 1932 was a sixteen-year-old girl. Her account of Sunday 18 September 1932 has survived, although, sadly, not her name. She recalls how the ramblers set off to walk the three and a half miles (five kilometres) from Sheffield to the starting point: 'we got plenty of stares as we marched along, singing Woodcraft and "bolshie" songs.' The Woodcraft Folk (see pages 75–6) has long been active in Sheffield, and several of the trespassers were young people from that organization.

She continues that when they reached the starting point at the ancient boundary ditch of the Bar Dike they were told to keep together and not to give their names if arrested. 'When we arrived at the beginning of the moors, two gamekeepers were there, with a man on the bike. A gamekeeper advised us to go back, and as we went straight on, he sent the cyclist with a message, we presume, to get assistance.'

The trespassers now faced about five miles (eight kilometres) of rough moorland walking, through tussocky grass and bogs along Hurkling Edge and across Flint Hill. When they got to Peter's Rock, a point overlooking Abbey Brook, they met about forty gamekeepers, among whom were a few policemen.

Here, as they paused to discuss what to do next, the gamekeepers advanced on them wielding pit props. The young girl recalls: 'Two lads got it worse than any of us, as one refused to give his name and address. After much discussion and argument, we set off back across the way we had come, accompanied this time by the police and the gamekeepers, who kept urging us on. I am sure they must have enjoyed their five-mile walk on a Sunday afternoon. We shall make them into ramblers yet!'

Just a few weeks earlier, at the Derby Assizes in July 1932, prison sentences of up to six months had been handed down to five of the ramblers taking part in the Kinder trespass, a heavy-handed response which served to antagonize the outdoor movement. Perhaps significantly, this time there were to be no arrests. The ramblers certainly believed they had made their point. 'It was a full day of excitement although we had to turn back,' recalled the girl. 'But numbers make a difference. Next time we want a thousand, not two hundred.'

But perhaps she and her fellow ramblers that day were not really trespassers at all. G.H.B. Ward took a keen interest in this path and decided to research its history. This led him to look in detail at the provisions of the Ecclesfield Tithes and Enclosure Act of 1811 – which, according to Ward, laid down that the Duke of Norfolk's Road was a public road all were entitled to use.

WALK 4

MARGERY HILL AND DERWENT EDGE

DIFFICULTY 👢 👢 👢 👢 👢

DISTANCE 13 miles (20.9 km)

| FAIRHOLMES | WILFREY NIELD | MARGERY HILL | BACK TOR | DOVESTONE TOR | DERWENT VILLAGE |
| ABBEY BROOK | HOWDEN EDGE | ROUND HILL | DERWENT EDGE | WHEEL STONES | FAIRHOLMES |

MAPS OS Explorer 287, West Pennine Moors; OS Explorer OL1, The Peak District – Dark Peak area

STARTING POINT National Park visitor centre at Fairholmes (GR 172893)

PARKING In the car parks at Fairholmes

PUBLIC TRANSPORT Buses from Sheffield and Glossop. A minibus runs to the head of the valley at King's Tree at weekends and bank holidays, when the road is closed to traffic.

This tough moorland hike ascends from the forest-cloaked reservoirs of the Derwent valley to the heights of Margery Hill, Round Hill and Derwent Edge, taking in oddities such as the natural rock 'window' called Wilfrey Nield and the exotically named tors of Derwent Edge – the Cakes of Bread, the Salt Cellar and the Coach and Horses.

▶ We start this long and quite strenuous day's walk from the

National Park visitor centre at Fairholmes.

■ Originally a farm, Fairholmes was used as a masons' workyard during the construction of the Derwent and Howden reservoir dams in 1901–17. The building of the Derwent dams was a major feat of civil engineering. A thousand navvies lived in a workmen's village known as Tin Town at Birchinlee, a mile (1.6 km) up the valley road by the side of the Derwent reservoir (see page 65).

▶ Take the road which leads down beneath the towering Derwent dam, which in times of high rainfall overflows in an awesome waterfall. From the right-hand corner of the dam wall, take the steps which lead up through the trees to the perimeter track around the reservoir ❶.

■ The Derwent and Howden reservoirs were built to supply water to the cities of Derby, Nottingham, Leicester and Sheffield. The Derwent was the second to be completed, in 1916, and in the Second World War was the scene of training runs made by the famous 617 Squadron, the Dambusters, in preparation for their attack on the Ruhr valley dams in 1943.

▶ Continue along the shore road through Shireowlers Wood, with the site of the workmen's village of Birchinlee in the trees under Birchinlee Pasture on the opposite shore. As the towers of the Howden dam appear ahead, the track descends towards the Abbey Brook Bridge ❷. Cross the bridge and immediately turn right and up the track which ascends through the trees of Hey Bank and out on to the open moor.

Climb up on the track past the summit of Nether Hey at 1365 ft (416 m) to your left and continue as the track degenerates into a path leading across the wastes of Upper Hey towards the rocky escarpment of Howden Edge.

■ Between the boggy crossings of Little Cranberry Clough and Sandy Lee Clough, among the rocks of Wilfrey Edge to the right,

▶ page 58

Derwent dam

some searching will reveal the extraordinary natural feature known as Wilfrey Nield or Needle ❸. A block of gritstone has fallen out of a buttress springing from the edge, creating this natural 'window'. It is named after the 'squint', or narrow passageway, in St Wilfrid's cell in the crypt of Ripon Cathedral. Local lads were once challenged to crawl through Wilfrey Nield to prove their manhood (although at Ripon squeezing through the squint was claimed to indicate chastity).

▶ Passing under Howden Edge, you soon meet the Cut Gate track descending from Featherbed Moss. Turn right here, along the path, and then left on top of the edge to gain the peaty, boulder-strewn summit of Margery Hill, at 1791 ft (546 m) the highest point of the walk and in South Yorkshire (GR 189957) ❹.

Now head south along the top of Wilfrey Edge on a path which swings south-east towards the summit of Round Hill (GR 204939) ❺ and, just beyond that, the Duke's Road (see Walk 3).

© Crown Copyright 100043293 2004

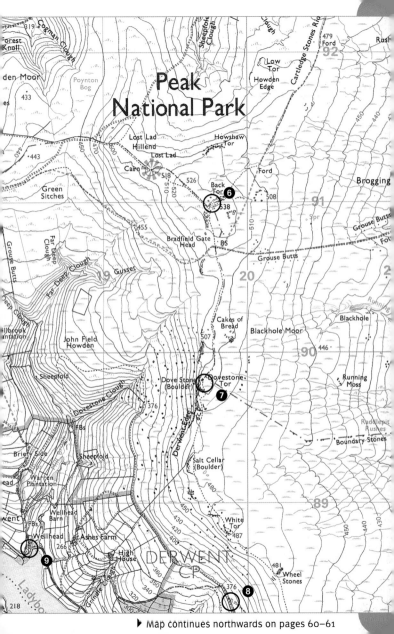

Peak
National Park

▶ Map continues northwards on pages 60–61

Keep heading south along the Cartledge Stones Ridge, following a boundary ditch which after another boggy mile (1.6 km) reaches the prominent rocks of Back Tor, one of the finest and wildest viewpoints in the Dark Peak (GR 197910) ❻.

■ The summit of Back Tor at 1765 ft (538 m) – the trig point is actually cemented on to the topmost tor – was one of the favourite places of John Derry, author of the bog-trotters' classic *Across the Derbyshire Moors*, first published in 1904. He wrote:

It is a wild, wide place, far from the ways of men, who here are the most occasional of creatures, and all its notes have the sadness of great spaces – of the mountains, moors, and seas. And yet it does one good to get into this upland, age-long solitude, where the primeval world is felt to be a mighty fact, linked on to us. The spirit of the moors has his throne on Back Tor.

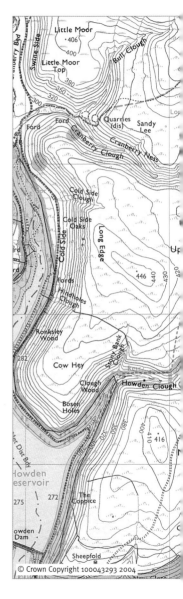

© Crown Copyright 100043293 2004

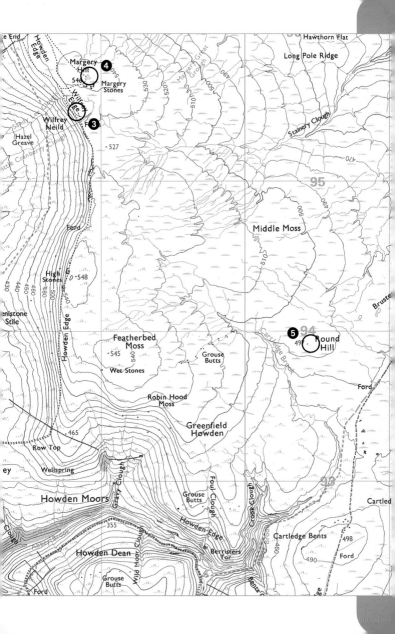

The view extends north to the wilderness of Bleaklow and the head of the Derwent valley, and south-west to the Kinder plateau. To the south there's a glimpse of the Ladybower reservoir and the craggy summit of Win Hill breaks the horizon at the end of the Great Ridge, while to the east across Strines can be seen the white tower blocks of the city of Sheffield, something Derry would not have seen.

▶ Keep heading south on a flagged path through the peat and heather towards the next outcrop, known as the Cakes of Bread. Dovestone Tor **7** is then the next of these gritstone remnants which, unlike the softer rock that once surrounded them, have survived the ravages of erosion.

Go south again on the paved path and you soon reach the anvil-shaped Salt Cellar, which stands in glorious isolation in a sea of heather to the right. Cross White Tor and head towards the prominent large outcrop known as the Wheel Stones or the Coach and Horses.

Just below the Coach and Horses, at the crossroads of the edge path and the bridleway which leads to Moscar **8**, turn right to reach a gate giving on to open country. Follow the path down above a plantation wall to Grindle Clough, past a collection of recently restored barns, one of which has a lintel dated 1647. From the barns, the path is again paved as it leads down to the road around the eastern shore of the Ladybower reservoir **9**.

■ The Ladybower was the last of the Derwent valley reservoirs to be built, between 1935 and 1943, and necessitated the depopulation of the twin villages of Ashopton and Derwent. In times of drought, the foundations of part of Derwent village are sometimes revealed in the reservoir floor. The reservoir was opened by King George VI in 1945.

▶ Turn right on the eastern perimeter road to walk the last mile (1.6 km) back to

Fairholmes, passing the gateposts to Derwent Hall and what remains of Derwent village, now a few farmsteads clustered around a telephone box. The road eventually swings beneath the towers of the Derwent dam to return to Fairholmes.

Derwent Edge

Tip's vigil

The story of shepherd Joseph Tagg and his faithful sheepdog Tip grabbed the public imagination at the close of the severe winter which marked the end of Coronation Year, 1953.

Joe, for forty years one of the Duke of Norfolk's shepherds in the upper Derwent valley, was one of the best-known and most respected shepherds in the country, and the winner of many sheepdog trials throughout Britain. Born at Ronksley Farm (later to be submerged under the waters of the Howden reservoir), Joe was now eighty-six and retired, and he kept his favourite dog Tip, an eleven-year-old collie bitch, as a companion.

On the snowy afternoon of 12 December, Joe was seen walking up the upper Derwent towards Slippery Stones with Tip at his side. When he did not return that night, the alarm was raised and gamekeepers, farmers, relatives and mountain rescue teams started searching the misty, snow-covered moors for him. No sign was found.

January and February were equally cold and snowy, and memories of Joe and Tip started to fade. It was not until 27 March that an employee of the Water Board, who was helping a farmer round up sheep on Ronksley Moor, discovered Tip in an emaciated condition a few yards from the body of her master. Tip had worn a path around Joe's body as she kept up her lonely three-month vigil.

It was thought that Joe had gone back to visit the site of his old childhood home and had then wandered up Westend Clough. Tip was carried off the moor and became a national heroine, awarded the top RSPCA animal bravery medal. She lived on for two more years before dying in February 1955.

A gravestone to the memory of Tip was raised by public subscription beside the Derwent dam – a touching reminder of the faithfulness of Man's best friend.

Memories of Tin Town

Little now remains of the navvies' village of Birchinlee, where a thousand workers and their families lived for fifteen years while the mighty Derwent and Howden dams were being constructed in the early years of the twentieth century. Just the vague outlines of a couple of terraces can be discerned among the trees on the western side of the Derwent reservoir above Ouzelden Clough, marking the place where 'Tin Town' stood.

The local nickname referred to the fact that the walls of the workmen's huts were of corrugated iron – the cheapest building material available at the time. But the interiors of the bungalows were anything but Spartan, lined with wood and heated by coal-burning grates to withstand the harsh Peak District winters.

The community was almost completely self-sufficient, with its own shops, school, public house, hospital, recreation hall and grounds, and police station. It was linked to the outside world by a railway, constructed to bring stone to the dam sites, which ran to Bamford and the Sheffield line three or four times a day.

Tin Town had a vigorous social life with two football teams and a cricket eleven which played other teams in the Hope valley and beyond. Social life revolved around the recreation hall, where there were billiard tables and a well-stocked library financed by profits from the Derwent Canteen, the only building in the village licensed to sell alcohol. Regular concerts were held in the hall, along with whist drives, dances, hand-cranked film showings and an annual horticultural show.

But Tin Town's future was always limited, and by 1912, with the completion of the Howden dam and the impending completion of Derwent, its days were numbered. Demolition of the huts began in December 1913 as the navvies moved on to other projects, leaving behind them what were then the two largest masonry dams in the country as fine memorials.

WALK 5

BAMFORD AND STANAGE EDGES

DIFFICULTY 👟 👟 👟 👟   **DISTANCE 5 miles (8 km)**

MOSCAR — HORDRON EDGE — GREAT TOR — LONG CAUSEWAY — HIGH NEB — MOSCAR

CUTTHROAT BRIDGE — JARVIS CLOUGH — BAMFORD EDGE — STANAGE EDGE — STANAGE END

MAP OS Explorer OL1, The Peak District – Dark Peak area

STARTING POINT Moscar lay-by on the A57 east of Ladybower (GR 216874)

PARKING In the car park

PUBLIC TRANSPORT Buses from Glossop and Sheffield

Bamford Edge, and in particular Great Tor at its northern end, is one of the finest viewpoints in the Peak, but was previously barred to the walker. This moorland hike also takes in Stanage Edge, Bamford's eastern neighbour, which is a place of pilgrimage for rock climbers from all over Britain.

▶ Start the walk from the large lay-by on the A57 west of Nether Reever Low at Moscar.

■ That expert chronicler of the eastern moors Terry Howard has described Moscar as the Spaghetti Junction of old packhorse routes between Yorkshire and Derbyshire, and many hollow ways certainly seem to converge here to cross the Ladybower Brook, including Halifax Gate – the old road between Bakewell and Halifax. The lay-by is in a former quarry where the people of Hathersage Outseats were given the right to take stone under the Enclosure Acts of the early nineteenth century.

▶ Walk carefully down the A57 road to reach the trees near Cutthroat Bridge, and take the track which leads left (south) under Hordron Edge, passing close to the Hordron Edge stone circle (GR 215868) ❶ up on the moorland to your left.

■ Cutthroat Bridge, built when the Snake Road turnpike was constructed between 1820 and 1821, takes its bloodcurdling name from the fact that at some time during the sixteenth century a man was found murdered, with his throat cut, near an older bridge further up Highshaw Clough opposite.

The Hordron Edge circle is quite difficult to locate, especially when the bracken is high in the summertime. It probably dates from the Bronze Age (up to 4000 years

ago), when this area of Bamford Moor and much of the other relatively flat land above the steep gritstone edges was cultivated, with clearance cairns (piles of stones left behind when the land was cleared) and extensive field systems. The climate was warmer in those days and the soil not so impoverished as it is today.

▶ Continue south-east along the vehicle track which leads into Jarvis Clough, where there is a shooting cabin at a convenient crossing point. Following another old hollow way through a line of grouse butts, head due west towards the hut circle and field systems, again dating from the Bronze Age, which are marked on the map. You pass a deep depression known as the Pit, which is probably the remains of a former coal-mining bell pit.

Head for the northern end of Bamford Edge, seen in profile ahead, and gradually ascend, with increasingly good views towards the overhanging rocks of Great Tor (GR 207849) ❷. You are now at around 1300 ft (400 m).

■ This is one of the finest viewpoints in the whole of the Peak District, but was frustratingly out of bounds until the new access legislation. There is an almost aerial view of the grass-covered, earthen embankment of the Ladybower reservoir in the foreground, with the white arches of the Ashopton viaduct beyond, striding across the northern arm of the reservoir. The twin-topped summits of Crook Hill and craggy Win Hill are prominent above the viaduct, with the blue whaleback of Bleaklow beyond and the tor-topped heights of Derwent Edge (Walk 4) to the left. To the south, there are views down the length of the Derwent valley over Bamford, and up to Offerton Moor and the prominent radio mast on Shatton Moor.

▶ Continue east along this glorious promenade which now swings south-east. More cairns and enclosures are marked on the heather moorland to your left. When the rocks of the edge peter

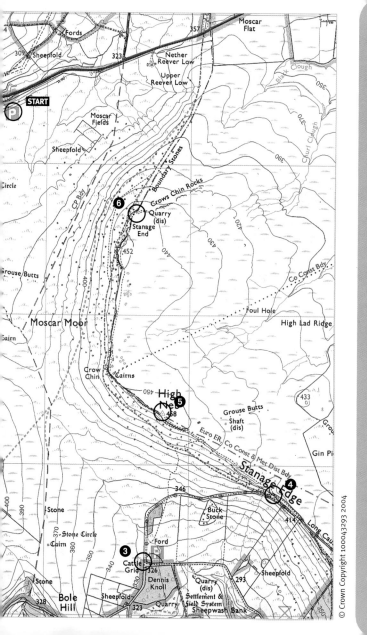

out, head eastwards across the moor, passing a small quarry where millstones were once worked, towards the long line of crags of Stanage Edge.

You eventually meet the minor road at the cattle grid near the Dennis Knoll plantation ❸, where you take the walled track leading off to the left. This swings round another small plantation and then heads due east, passing the enclosed boulders which include the Buck Stone on the right.

■ This ancient route is known as the Long Causeway, and is said to be Roman in origin. When it was in use as a paved packhorse way it linked Sheffield with the Hope valley, climbing through the crags of Stanage Edge to the south of High Neb.

Stanage Edge ❹ is usually festooned with the bright colours of climbers' ropes and their equally bright clothing, while hang-gliders

Great Tor, Bamford Edge

and parascenders soar above like modern-day pterodactyls. Stanage is one of the most famous climbing crags in the world, where working-class heroes such as Joe Brown and Don Whillans pushed the art of climbing to new levels of skill and daring in the 1950s, before going on to conquer Himalayan giants. The first climbs here were made by Sheffield silversmith J.W. Puttrell in the later years of the nineteenth century, so Stanage could be regarded as the birthplace of modern rock climbing. At the last count, there were upwards of 850 climbing routes along this 3-mile (5-km) long, 80-ft (25-m) high wall of highly abrasive gritstone.

A large flat rock below Stanage Edge is known as the 'Rock of Resolution' to local members of the progressive youth movement, the Woodcraft Folk (see pages 75–6). It was here, under the leadership of Basil Rawson, that the decision was taken in 1929 to create the first Woodcraft Folk groups in the North.

The views from the escarpment top of Stanage are equally extensive as, and slightly higher than, those from Bamford Edge, taking in the distant shapes of Kinder Scout and Bleaklow, with the broad, bracken-covered expanse of Bamford Moor forming the foreground. Win Hill is still prominent in front above the now invisible Ladybower reservoir.

▶ Turn left (north-west) to continue along the crest of Stanage to its crowning summit of High Neb at 1503 ft (458 m) **5**. Neb is a northern word meaning 'nose'. Walk on to Crow Chin where at two large burial cairns in the heather the edge turns north to reach Stanage End **6**, with the disused quarry at Crows Chin Rocks to the right.

Leave the edge here and descend across the rough moorland of Moscar Fields past an enclosed sheepfold to return to the lay-by and the starting point of the walk.

The mountain blackbird

Walkers enjoying the views from Stanage or Bamford Edge in the spring and early summer may well hear the flutey song or the harsh warning 'chack, chack' call of one of Britain's rarest songbirds – the ring ouzel or mountain blackbird.

From a distance, it looks like the familiar garden blackbird. On closer inspection, however, it can be seen that the male sports a gorgeous white crescent across its breast, like the gorget

Ring ouzel

worn by officers of the Household Cavalry. The female has a less distinct gorget but has a similar pale grey colouring to the male bird.

Known as a tor ouzel on Dartmoor, where this summer visitor from the Atlas Mountains and the Mediterranean frequents a similar habitat, the ring ouzel has given its name to several physical features of the Dark Peak, including Ouzelden Clough in the upper Derwent valley.

The return of the ring ouzel to the crags and moors of Stanage Edge has been a triumph of co-operation between the landowners (the Peak District National Park authority), the nature conservationists and the walkers, climbers, hang-gliders and parascenders who use the crag, which is one of the busiest in Britain.

The British population of ring ouzels – already on the Red List of threatened species – had plummeted by more than fifty per cent over the last decade. Stanage was one of their last strongholds, but two successful nest sites were right in the middle of the popular climbing area. Through the good work of the Stanage Forum, a voluntary group which comprises all users of the crag and the area around it, visitors have been encouraged to avoid these areas during the crucial four-week period from the time the birds build their nests until the chicks are fledged. The result has been an encouraging increase in the number of ring ouzels on the site.

The Stanage Forum, along with the Park's 'Moors for the Future' project, is a fine example of different user groups working together for the common good, and the unmistakable and characteristic sight and sound of the ring ouzel back on the crags is everyone's reward.

The Woodcraft Folk

On 14 April 1929, a small group of nine young people led by local Independent Labour Party secretary Basil Rawson set off from Sheffield for a hike to Stanage Edge. 'They had something to discuss and decide, and for that needed privacy and "atmosphere",' as Rawson was to write later.

The group found the atmosphere they wanted on the rocky slopes below windswept Stanage Edge, where after lunch they had a pow-wow on a large flat stone, which later became celebrated in Woodcraft Folk tradition as the 'Rock of Resolution'.

The resolution the group decided on that momentous day was to set up the Sheffield branch of the radical youth movement known as the Woodcraft Folk.

The Woodcraft Folk had been established in south London in 1925 by nineteen-year-old Leslie Paul, as a socialist and co-operative alternative to the more militaristic Scout movement. (The term 'woodcraft' was used by the influential writer and naturalist Ernest Thompson Seton at the turn of the twentieth century to mean the skill of living in the open air, close to nature.) Rawson had seen an article written by Leslie Paul in the *New Leader* newspaper of December 1928 which suggested the need to develop such an organization for young people. Rawson himself at this time was, as he put it, 'disappointed at the apparent slowness of political progress' being made by the Left, and was inspired by Paul's article to do something about it. The Stanage meeting was the result.

'A small band of colleagues – they pledged themselves to "carry the torch of Woodcraft" into the streets of the Steel City, and to rally an ever-growing company of boys and girls who would break a new trail – to a new world,' he later explained. Rawson became a key figure in the Woodcraft Folk, known in the movement by his 'folk name' of 'Brown Eagle'.

The Woodcraft Folk is still going strong today, describing itself as 'an educational movement for young people, designed to develop self-confidence and activity in society, with the aim of building a world based on equality, peace, social justice and co-operation'. The movement encourages young people to enjoy the outdoor life through camping and hostelling trips and the study of nature. Today there are about four hundred groups, mainly based in urban areas of Britain, where weekly meetings are held involving games, drama, craft, singing and dancing. Sheffield remains one of the movement's strongest centres in northern England.

Young members of the Woodcraft Folk at camp in the 1930s

WALK 6

BURBAGE MOOR AND CARL WARK

DIFFICULTY 🥾 🥾 🥾 **DISTANCE About 7 miles (11 km)**

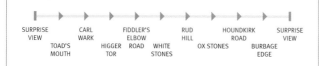

SURPRISE VIEW — TOAD'S MOUTH — CARL WARK — HIGGER TOR — FIDDLER'S ELBOW ROAD — WHITE STONES — RUD HILL — OX STONES — HOUNDKIRK ROAD — BURBAGE EDGE — SURPRISE VIEW

MAP OS Explorer OL1, The Peak District – Dark Peak area

STARTING POINT Surprise View car park on the A6187 (GR 252801)

PARKING In the car park

PUBLIC TRANSPORT Buses from Sheffield

Hathersage Moor offers walkers the chance to study the landscape of tor formation, with Higger Tor and Carl Wark perhaps the best-known features. This moorland ramble also takes in the Hallam Moors, which were previously out of bounds, and returns over Dore Moor and Houndkirk Moor.

▶ The walk starts from the National Park car park at Surprise View, just above the quarried escarpment of Millstone Edge and a view down the Hope valley on the road to Hathersage. Immediately to the north are the tors of Mother Cap and Over Owler, well worth exploring for the grand view down the valley.

Walk along the A6187 in a north-easterly direction (towards Sheffield) for ½ mile (0.8 km)

until you reach the famous landmark known as Toad's Mouth ❶. This is a gritstone boulder which overhangs the road near Burbage Bridge. Someone has carved an eye on it to produce the unmistakable look of the warty amphibian.

Take the obvious track which leads north from here through the heather towards the mysterious rocky hilltop of Carl Wark ❷ (see page 84), which many consider to be an ancient fortification and which may be Iron Age or even earlier. Note the massive wall at the western entrance, and spend a little time exploring this prehistoric enigma.

■ The overhanging rock on the north side of the enclosure is known as Caer's Chair, and it is traditional to sit in it to admire the view across towards Higger Tor and down to the plantations in the valley of the Burbage Brook below.

▶ Now take the obvious and eroded path towards the height

of Higger Tor (GR 257820) ❸, with its conspicuous leaning block prominent to the left of the escarpment.

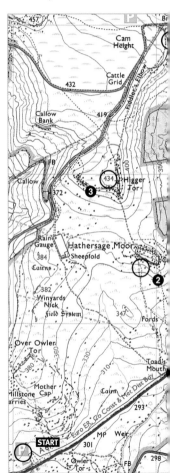

■ This tor is popular with rock climbers and the climbs on it, although not long (50 ft/15 m), are quite demanding, with descriptive names such the Rasp and the File – an indication of the abrasive nature of the Chatsworth grit

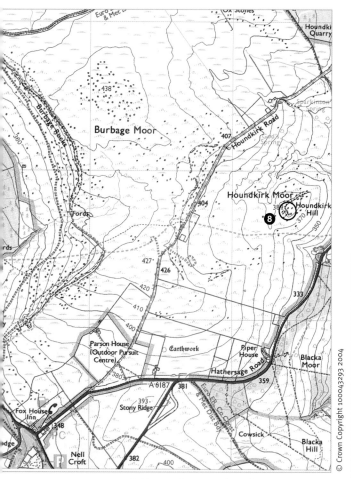

© Crown Copyright 100043293 2004

▶ Map continues northwards on pages 80–81

hereabouts. The summit of Higger Tor is 1424 ft (434 m).

▶ Now contour north alongside the Fiddler's Elbow Road to Upper Burbage Bridge ❹, where there are usually refreshments available in the summer season.

The route now heads due north again across the open moor, crossing Friar's Ridge, an ancient boundary line across White Path Moss, to reach the scattered rocks of White Stones ❺. These probably take their name, like White Edge, from the White family of Tedgness Farm in Grindleford.

Turn east, with fine views ahead across the city of

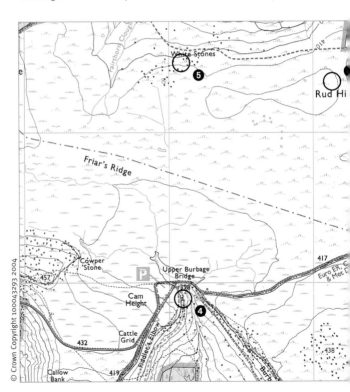

© Crown Copyright 100043293 2004

Sheffield, to reach Rud Hill ❻, where there are the remains of a stone shelter. The quarry on Brown Edge above Brown Edge Farm is now immediately below you. At this point head south to cross the Ringinglow Road west of Lady Canning's Plantation.

Still heading south, make for the trig point on Ox Stones at 1375 ft (419 m) ❼, another fine viewpoint across Sheffield to the east.

Follow the broken-down wall between the rocks to the ruins of Badger House on the old Houndkirk Road, also known as the Sheep Track. Crossing the walled road, head for the spring known as God's Spring, where the water is clear and pure.

The rocky little escarpment of Houndkirk Hill (GR 284818) ❽ is the next objective and is yet another fine viewpoint. Houndkirk Hill can be considered as a series of tors in formation, with the softer rock gradually weathering away around the upstanding tors of harder Chatsworth grit.

Now head west across the moor and across Houndkirk Road again towards the natural amphitheatre created by the Burbage Brook and the edge of Burbage Rocks. This gives a grand aerial view across the plantations in the valley bottom to Carl Wark and Higger Tor.

It is now a short step south back to Burbage Bridge and Toad's Mouth, and the car park at Surprise View.

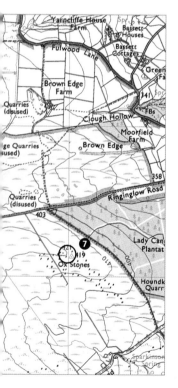

Stanage Edge from Higger Tor

The mystery of Carl Wark

The mysterious gritstone tor and structure known as Carl Wark, on the moors above Hathersage, has puzzled archaeologists for centuries. Situated on a natural outcrop below and to the south of Higger Tor, it has variously been described as a neolithic settlement, an Iron Age hill fort, a Druid temple and even as a folly. Whatever it was originally, this strangely isolated rock-rimmed height continues to fascinate visitors and, until a proper investigation is made, will continue to keep its secrets.

Even the name, Carl Wark, excites controversy. Some say it means the structure was the work of the Caels, or Gaels, the early Celtic settlers, while others point out that the overhanging rock with a large hollow in it (found on the north side of the site) is known as Caer's Chair, and therefore by association the Cyclopean dry-stone enclosing rampart on the western end was Caer's Work.

Certainly there is nothing else in northern England like this ten-foot (three-metre) high wall of huge slabs and boulders. Small cliffs of Chatsworth grit form natural defences on each of the other three sides. The apparently defensive nature of the site has caused Carl Wark to be most often described as an Iron Age hill fort. But, if this was the case, why did the builders not choose a higher and strategically more sensible site at Higger Tor to the north? No conclusive evidence of settlement has been found in the interior of the Carl Wark enclosure, which in any case is strewn with large, earth-fast boulders.

Because Carl Wark stands close to a well-documented landscape, to the south and west, of clearance cairns and field systems from the first millennium BC, the latest archaeological thinking seems to be that it may in fact be a much earlier site, perhaps dating to neolithic times or the Bronze Age.

A worthy SCAM

Inspired by G.H.B. Ward and the early trespassers, the Sheffield Campaign for Access to Moorland (SCAM) is one of the leading campaigning bodies which fought for the freedom to roam.

This voluntary organization evolved from celebrations in 1982 marking the fiftieth anniversary of the mass trespass on Kinder Scout. A group of Sheffield activists felt that the events gave a renewed emphasis to the fight for access to moorland, and challenged the assumption that, with the introduction of access agreements, the battle was won.

The lack of official progress being made towards the right to roam freely in open country was frustrating the Sheffielders, just as it had the trespassers of the 1930s. The right to walk freely on the moors, SCAM felt, was part of the Steel City's cultural and social heritage.

SCAM organized mass trespasses over the then still forbidden moors to the west of Sheffield and in 1988 even issued *Freedom of the Moors,* a booklet describing ten 'alternative' rambles in the Peak District which all involved trespassing. Many of the walks in this book follow all or part of the routes given in SCAM's booklet. SCAM was represented on the Peak District Local Access Forum, the body which helped draw up the new 'conclusive' maps showing access land.

In the preface to *Freedom of the Moors*, the organization expressed its philosophy: 'SCAM supporters, along with many other ramblers and outdoor users, are responsible and concerned people. We believe that what is needed and should be achievable is an integrated system of access which would benefit both the wildlife and the walker.'

At a meeting shortly after the passing of the Countryside and Rights of Way Act 2000, SCAM resolved to continue as a campaigning organization.

WALK 7

BIG MOOR AND SWINE STY

DIFFICULTY 👢 👢 👢 **DISTANCE About 5 miles (8 km)**

UPPER LONGSHAW — WHITE EDGE — SWINE STY — BARBROOK — BARBROOK RESERVOIR — LADY'S CROSS — UPPER LONGSHAW

MAP OS Explorer OL24, The Peak District – White Peak area

STARTING POINT Upper Longshaw car park, on the A625 south of Hathersage (GR 267790)

PARKING In the National Trust car park

PUBLIC TRANSPORT Buses from Sheffield

Big Moor is exactly what its name says it is – a 10-square-mile (25-sq-km) wilderness of open moorland. It was acquired by the National Park from the Severn Trent water authority in 1984 and has been managed as a wildlife refuge. Access by walkers was not encouraged except on footpaths, but under the new access legislation it becomes open to all again.

▶ The walk starts from the National Trust's Upper Longshaw car park above the Longshaw Estate. It is near the Wooden Pole, a regularly replaced landmark at the junction of a number of ancient cross-moor hollow ways. Take the bridleway which leads south across White Edge Moor towards the Hurkling Stone at the end of the rocky White Edge escarpment ❶.

■ White Edge, according to
G.H.B. Ward, takes its name
not from the fluffy white
fruiting heads of cotton grass
so common on Big Moor
but from the White family of

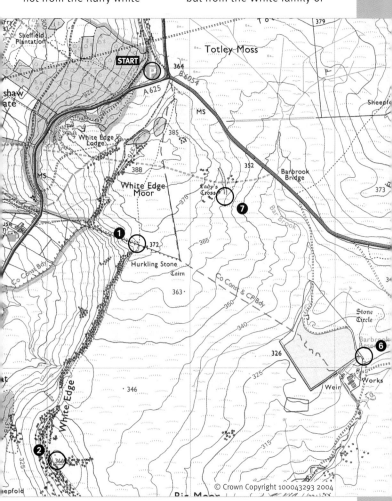

© Crown Copyright 100043293 2004

▶ Map continues southwards on page 88

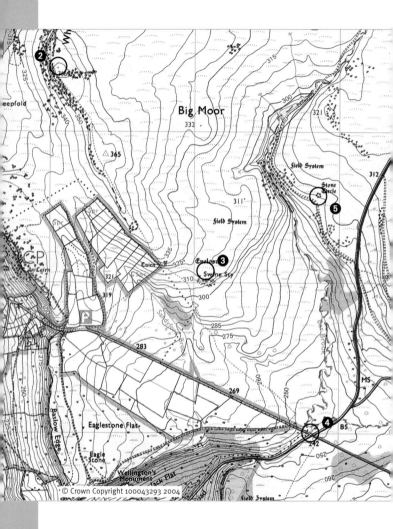

Tedgness Farm, Grindleford. A hurkling stone means locally a stone that is crouching or bending, or one that has been hurled or thrown.

In the 1927/28 *Clarion Handbook*, Ward describes Big Moor thus: 'It is big and brown, wide and drear, featureless and lonely, flat and boggy as any moor in Peakland, and yet, to those who known it most intimately, full of interest, and, in the treading of it, verily, a big man's moor.'

There are fine views across the Derwent valley to Froggatt, Curbar and Calver from the summit of White Edge (GR 261764) at 1200 ft (366 m) ❷, with the gash of Stoney Middleton Gorge biting into the limestone plateau beyond. Evidence of a lead-smelting site has been discovered near the top of White Edge. The site was obviously placed here to take advantage of the frequent westerly winds blowing up from the valley below, creating a strong draught for the smelting hearth.

▶ Continue to follow the heather-clad escarpment south until it narrows to a ridge which dies out at an ancient burial cairn west of the prehistoric settlement of Swine Sty (GR 271750) ❸, on the downward slope of the moor to the left. The hut and stone circles stand out in green islands of closely grazed grass amid the bracken and coarse moorgrass.

■ The settlement of Swine Sty was originally dated to the early Bronze Age, but the latest interpretation of the flint artefacts found there suggests an earlier, late neolithic date (*c.* 3000–2000 BC). It was certainly also occupied into the later Bronze Age and Iron Age, judging from the pottery that has been discovered in the area. Associated with the stone foundations of the buildings are stone circles, burial cairns and field systems, indicating a complete prehistoric landscape to rival those on Dartmoor. The settlement seems to have existed for several hundred years.

In addition to the domestic artefacts which have been recovered from the site, there is evidence to suggest a small cottage industry making decorative polished-shale rings or bracelets.

▶ After exploring the Swine Sty settlement, continue southwards down the ridge to the clapper bridge which crosses the Bar Brook near the junction of the A621 Sheffield road with a number of minor roads ❹.

■ This double-slabbed clapper bridge was on the packhorse route between the Hope valley and Baslow via Curbar Gap to Chesterfield, which was turnpiked in 1759. One of the slabs, which measure 9 ft (2.7 m), is inscribed on its side with the date 1777 preceded by the letter 'H' (probably referring to the Holmesfield parish boundary), and on its top surface with the date 1742.

▶ Now we follow, on its eastern bank, the meandering course of the Bar Brook northwards through thin woodland, to climb up and join a track coming from the right.

■ This track leads close to another of the area's prehistoric wonders, a small reconstructed stone circle dating from the Bronze Age, found in the encircling heather overlooking the brook ❺. The irregular ring of stones is set inside a dry-stone wall on the inner edge of an earth and rubble bank, with an entrance to the north-west. Four cremations have been excavated from the interior, one in a stone burial box known as a kist.

The circle stands near a large cairnfield on the edge of Ramsley Moor, where field systems also dating from the Bronze Age have been identified, near to an old guide stoop.

▶ A track now leads north, alongside an old stone causeway, across the moor towards Barbrook reservoir ❻ and its associated works, where there is yet another circle of fairly insignificant stones on its northern edge.

Clapper bridge over Bar Brook, Big Moor

■ Barbrook reservoir and its two embankments were built in 1908 to supply water to Chesterfield. It covers an area of about 30 acres, is 34 ft (10 m) deep and contains around 100 million gallons of water.

▶ From here head north-west to cross the Bar Brook as it flows into the reservoir by another clapper bridge, near Barbrook Bridge on the B6054. Now take the footpath leading back on to the moor, through the rocks and heather, to the landmark known as Lady's Cross (GR 272782) ❼.

■ Stumpy Lady's Cross, which rises from a square base of gritstone, was first mentioned in 1263, and stands where the Hope valley to Chesterfield, and Sheffield to Tideswell packhorse routes crossed. It probably once marked the western boundary of the estate belonging to the Premonstratensian monks of Beauchief Abbey near Sheffield (this religious order, also known as the White Canons, takes its name from the town in France where it was founded early in the twelfth century). Later the cross was used to mark the junction of the boundaries of Hathersage, Holmesfield and Totley parishes.

Writing in the *Clarion Handbook* of 1915/16, G.H.B. Ward wrote of Lady's Cross, 'You would run all the risks and penalties of trespass if you went to see it. Yet it should be a national monument and be well protected and railed off, for anyone to see and to learn from it; because it gives good history and education to any tramp.'

▶ It is now a short step north-west to regain the road and return to the car park.

Tom Tomlinson
– the Lone Ranger

There's an apocryphal story about how Tom Tomlinson of Hathersage, the first full-time National Park warden in Britain, used to test prospective volunteer wardens.

He'd take them out for a walk from Edale, setting off with his deceptively leisurely gait but enormously long strides up The Nab, a southern outlier of Kinder. If the would-be warden kept up with him and could still answer his questions at the top, they were in.

Tom Tomlinson became a legend in the outdoor world and he shared his vast knowledge of the moors and sense of respect for them among generations of young people through his entertaining guided walks. He was the pioneer from whom today's highly professional team of twenty-six full-time rangers, backed by an army of about 350 part-time volunteers at weekends, developed to cover the whole of the 555-square-mile (1437-sq-km) National Park. Rangers are often described as 'the eyes and ears of the Park', and Tom Tomlinson was the man who first opened those eyes and ears.

Tom was born in the mill town of Rossendale in Lancashire in 1908 and he started his working life as a trainee Baptist minister, working for two years in the East End of London. He returned to preach in his home town and later played for Burnley Football Club as an amateur.

But his love of the hills often took him to what was to become his spiritual home of Edale, and he claimed to have taken part in the mass trespass on Kinder in 1932. On his marriage to Hilda Crabtree, he became, like her, a Quaker and pacifist and the couple were appointed wardens of Edale Youth Hostel at Rowland Cote, Edale, in 1946.

He was appointed the first Chief Warden of the recently constituted Peak District National Park ten years later, with the simple job description that he would have to walk about twenty miles (thirty-two kilometres) a day, mainly on the newly negotiated access moors of Kinder and Bleaklow. He soon became well respected by both visitors and local people, and was an accomplished local historian, writing several booklets about the history of the Hathersage area. He became parish clerk of Hathersage in 1956.

Tom was also well known for his fondness for a cup of tea (he was a lifelong teetotaller), setting another tradition in the Ranger Service. One Christmas he was presented with a very large tea mug by Tom Cooper, owner of the legendary Cooper's Tea Rooms in Edale, with the words: 'To Tom, the talking teapot, the fastest drinker of tea in the valley'.

Tom retired in 1973 after seventeen years with the National Park and embarked on another career as a school teacher, first at Sheffield and later at Nottinghamshire County Council's Field Studies Centre in Hathersage, where he was once described as 'a sort of Hans Christian Andersen' to the children.

In his later years, Tom was registered blind and confined to an old people's home in Bakewell. He died at the age of eighty-seven in 1995.

The adder's dance

The most likely place in the Peak District to see Britain's only poisonous snake – the adder – is on Big Moor.

Although the most numerous of three species of snake found in Britain, adders are extremely shy and evasive creatures, usually disappearing into the heather at the approach of a rambler long before they can be seen. The adder is rather a squat snake with dark zigzag markings along its silvery yellow-brown back and a distinctive inverted V or X on the back of its head.

The name is interesting because it originally comes from the Anglo-Saxon *noedre* or *naedre*, which means 'creeping thing'. The word was corrupted to 'a nadder', becoming the modern 'an adder' (the Germans still use the word 'natter' for a type of snake). The Latin term for the adder is *Vipera berus*, which is thought to mean 'live-bearing snake' as the adder gives birth to

A pair of adders

live young, not eggs like the other British snakes, the grass snake and the smooth snake.

Usually, an adder will strike only if it feels seriously threatened or when it is feeding. And an adder's bite is very rarely fatal – you are more likely to die by being struck by lightning than from an adder's strike. Only around a dozen people have died from an adder's bite in the last eighty years. They usually feed on short-tailed field voles, lizards, nesting birds and birds' eggs, and hibernate in a hole in the ground during the winter.

One of the most compelling sights in nature is that of the fabled 'adders' dance'. This occurs during the spring when males are competing for females and territory. The males chase each other at surprisingly high speeds and then stop and aggressively rear up from the ground, swaying, ducking and weaving like two boxers, and occasionally intertwining until one is able to dominate the other.

The best advice for walking in adder country is just common sense: watch where you put your feet or where you sit on heathery or rocky ground, especially on warm and sunny days. And if you make plenty of noise as you walk by, the chances are you'll never even see a snake.

WALK 8

GARDOM'S EDGE AND LEASH FEN

DIFFICULTY 👟 👟 👟 **DISTANCE About 5 miles (8 km)**

| ROBIN HOOD PUBLIC HOUSE | GARDOM'S EDGE | BLAKE BROOK | LEASH FEN | WHIBBERSLEY CROSS | BIRCHEN EDGE | ROBIN HOOD PUBLIC HOUSE |

MAP OS Explorer OL24, The Peak District – White Peak area

STARTING POINT Car park near the Robin Hood public house on the A619 Baslow–Chesterfield road (GR 281721)

PARKING In the car park

PUBLIC TRANSPORT Buses from Chesterfield and Bakewell

The shelf of moorland which lies between Birchen Edge and Gardom's Edge has been described as a multi-period archaeological landscape, exhibiting features dating back to neolithic times. To the north-east, newly accessible Leash Fen is associated with legends of a long-lost township.

▶ Turn right and walk down the main road past the entrance to the Eric Byne campsite and take the stile on the right which leads up, the footpath crossing a number of hollow ways and passing a ring cairn dating from the Bronze Age. Over to the right are the scarcely visible remains of field systems dating from the same period.

The footpath eventually leads down through the woods to the Sheffield road (A621), but the route contours up right, towards

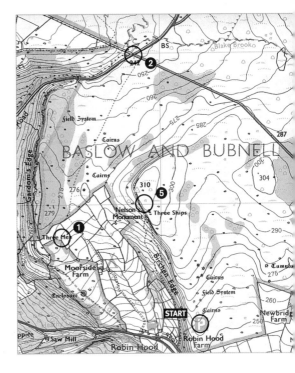

the prominent cairns which mark the southern end of Gardom's Edge ❶.

■ As you step on to the edge, you pass through a low, earthen embankment which can be followed as it sweeps around and encloses the southern end of Gardom's Edge. The large enclosure dates from the neolithic period (between 3500 and 2000 BC), and corresponds to causewayed enclosures found on the chalk downs of southern Britain, such as Windmill Hill near Avebury. It is the largest structure of its kind yet found in the north of England. Archaeologists believe these enclosures were built on the edge of communities and were associated with special ritual activities such as

© Crown Copyright 100043293 2004

feasting, exchanging goods and exposing the newly dead prior to the burial of their bones, a process that is known as excarnation.

Marked on the map as Three Men, the triple cairns on Gardom's Edge are apparently the remains of a Bronze Age barrow. There is a local tradition that they mark the burial places of three brothers from Baslow in the

valley below, but they later served as guide cairns to let travellers know where they could safely leave the edge and descend into the valley.

▶ Pass northwards along the edge, noting the medieval millstone quarries in the trees beneath the escarpment, and the hollow-way 'roads' which lead up through the edge, showing where millstones were rolled out and taken away after manufacture.

■ Among the several quarries in the rock face is one marked with the date 1803. A millstone-maker's smithy has been excavated here, and several unfinished or broken domed millstones can be found among the boulders, grooves in the rocks showing where chisels were sharpened.

▶ Now turn right above the edge to investigate the complete Bronze Age landscape which exists on the moor between the encroaching birches of the edge and the escarpment of Birchen Edge beyond.

■ Archaeologists have discovered whole field systems with associated clearance cairns, as well as ring cairns and barrows and standing stones (there is a particularly impressive one leaning among the trees near the edge), which show that thousands of years ago a community farmed, lived and died on these now inhospitable moors.

The most exciting feature of the Gardom's Edge landscape is undoubtedly the magnificent cup-and-ring-marked stone (see pages 104–5) which is found on a flat boulder just beyond the trees and outside the middle of the eastern bank of the neolithic enclosure. The stone you see is actually a fibreglass replica made by staff at Sheffield Museum, erected here to protect the actual stone, buried near by, from erosion and vandalism.

▶ After a thorough exploration of the Gardom's Edge prehistoric landscape, head north on a faint path through the heather which lleads to the crossroads of the A621 and the minor road between Old Brampton and Curbar Gap ❷. Walk along the Sheffield road for a few yards, before leaving it to follow the course of the Blake Brook (right), by an old boundary stone.

Follow the stream as it winds up through the heather, rough grass and birch scrub on to the wastes of Leash Fen – the only 'fen' and perhaps the flattest moor in the entire Peak ❸.

■ The legend attached to Leash Fen is that there was once a sizeable settlement here, perhaps echoing a long-lost folk memory of an Iron Age marsh fort built on wooden stilts. But there is no archaeological evidence to support this persistent folk tale. An old rhyme recounts:

When Leech-field was a market town,
Chesterfield was gorse and broom.
Now Chesterfield's a market town,
Leech-field a marsh is grown..

Leash Fen is now part of the National Park's Eastern Moors estate, acquired in 1984 and protected as a nature reserve, so please respect any wildlife you might see here and watch out for warning notices.

▶ Following the conduit which links Blake Brook with Blackleash Brook, heading due south-east from the centre of Leash Fen, make for spot height 288 m, marked on the map in scattered trees on the Curbar Gap–Old Brampton road. Turn left and head down the road until you see the stumpy, eroded remains of Whibbersley Cross (GR 294727) to the right ❹, another ancient guidepost to travellers crossing these featureless moors.

■ Whibbersley Cross is thought to date from the thirteenth century, and to have been erected as a boundary marker by the monks of Beauchief Abbey on the outskirts of modern Sheffield. Further down the road in the valley of the Blackleach Brook stands Clod Hall Farm. This unusual name relates to a former squatter's dwelling on the site, which was, as the name suggests, built of clods of earth or peat.

▶ Follow the enclosure walls westwards, crossing the open moor and passing more tumuli, clearance cairns and field systems dating from the Bronze Age, until after a rough ½ mile (0.8 km) you reach the top of the escarpment of Birchen Edge ❺, a favourite place for rock climbers.

■ Nelson's Monument, erected in 1805 to commemorate Nelson's victory at Trafalgar, is a popular belay point for rock climbers, although this use is not encouraged by the National Park authority. Immediately behind the monument are three isolated tors known as the Three Ships, and they carry the inscribed names of three of Lord Nelson's ships at Trafalgar – the Victory, the Reliance and the Royal Soverin (sic). The climbing routes on the escarpment beneath have appropriate nautical names such as the Crow's Nest, Kiss Me Hardy, Emma's Dilemma and Victory Crack.

▶ From Birchen Edge, follow the escarpment south to join the path which runs down to a stile on the B6050, where you turn right down the road and back to the Robin Hood car park.

Nelson's Monument

Rock art in the Peak

The enigmatic cup-and-ring markings pecked into boulders of gritstone which are such a common feature of the eastern Pennines from Northumberland to the Peak still retain their centuries-old secrets. For no one is quite sure how or why these intricate carvings were made, and there is even a dispute as to when this so-called 'rock art' was executed. Current thinking places them in the late neolithic period and early Bronze Age, about 4000–5000 years ago.

Perhaps the most spectacular example in the Peak is found on the boulder-strewn moor between Birchen and Gardom's Edge near Baslow, visited in Walk 8. Here a complicated pattern of concentric circles, twin rings each containing ten 'cups', and what looks like the shape of an eye have been carved into a massive boulder, which lies flat on the ground. One archaeologist has jokingly described it as looking like a Stone Age representation of the Hollywood cartoon character Snoopy.

What you see here today is not the original boulder, which was being badly eroded by the Peak District elements and at risk from vandalism, but a fibreglass cast taken from the original, which lies safely buried near by. It achieves its purpose of allowing the visitor to appreciate the setting of the stone, in the centre of a well-developed prehistoric landscape, which has been extensively investigated by archaeologists from the Peak District National Park and Sheffield University. They have identified the banks, field systems, clearance cairns, hut circles, ceremonial monuments and burial cairns of an extensive settlement dating back to the Bronze Age and before.

Other examples of rock art have been found in the surrounding area: on Ramsley Moor at Barbrook, on Eyam Moor, at Ball Cross above Bakewell (now in Sheffield Museum) and at Rowtor Rocks, near Birchover.

But why were these strange markings chipped out so patiently and carefully, presumably using stone implements? No one knows, although the latest thinking links them strongly to their position in the landscape where they are found. Rock art is often found in secret, hidden places, so maybe the markings were designed to be revealed to family members when they reached a certain age and were thought ready to learn the old truths. The swirling designs hint at what are known as entopic phenomena, associated with altered states of consciousness induced by taking hallucinatory substances or in trances experienced by people seeking visions or spiritual guidance.

The fibreglass replica of cup-and-ring markings at Gardom's Edge

Guide stoops –
signs of the times

Finding your way across the often featureless eastern moors of the Peak District is a problem modern bog-trotters have shared with travellers from the earliest times.

So both have benefited from the erection of standing stones at strategic points or junctions of routes to guide them. Collectively known as guide stoops, the earliest examples were boundary markers or crosses, such as Lady's Cross, Edale Cross and Hope Cross, which demarcated the boundaries of ancient forests or the vast monastic estates.

The majority of guide stoops found in the Peak, however, date from the eighteenth century, and followed an Act of Parliament of 1697. As well as setting out to improve the atrocious condition of turnpike roads, this Act also instructed Justices of the Peace to order the erection of guideposts or guidestones in moorland areas. The actual wording of the 1697 Act is addressed to the 'Surveyors of the Highways':

> in any parish or place where two or more cross highways meet, requiring them forthwith to cause to be erected or fixed, in a most convenient place where such ways join, a stone or post, with an inscription thereon in large letters, containing the name of the next market town to which each of the said joining highways leads . . .

The eastern moors of the Peak are particularly rich in these guide stoops (the term comes from the Old Scandinavian word for a stone). Travellers such as jaggers (packhorsemen), salters, hawkers, pedlars, tinkers and badgers (sellers of foodstuffs) would probably have been quite good at finding their way, but as trade increased between the manufacturing towns of Sheffield and Chesterfield and the places supplying raw materials (such as wool, lead, salt and stone) in the Peak District and beyond, the need for easily navigable routes became more important. The many occurrences of the name Saltergate in the Peak District area reflect the importance of the trade in Cheshire salt across the Pennines.

Many stoops seem to have been erected in a hurry, often using convenient blocks of gritstone found near at hand, and spelling is notoriously variable, probably reflecting the local dialect and pronunciation of the times. For example, there are no less than eight different spellings of Sheffield – ranging from 'Shafild' to 'Shefild' and 'Sheafield'. Similarly, Chesterfield was written as 'Chasterfeild', 'Chefterfield' and 'Chestterfeld', Tideswell as 'Tidsewall' or 'Tidswell', and Hathersage as 'Hatharsich'. Some stoops carry the date of their erection, and crudely carved hands or fingers pointing the way.

As turnpike roads started to provide safer crossings of the Pennines in the later eighteenth century, the importance of moorland guide stoops lessened and many fell into disrepair. Later, gamekeepers bent on deterring ramblers from walking across their owners' grouse moors deliberately took them down, re-used them as gateposts and, in some cases, destroyed or buried them.

The new interest in the past has seen several guide stoops re-erected as close as possible to their original position. Groups such as the Holymoorside Historical Society have been active in rescuing 'lost', buried or incorrectly placed stoops in places like Beeley Moor, East Moor and Elton Common.

Many of these 300-year-old 'signs of the times' are now listed by English Heritage, and recorded as treasures by the Peak District National Park authority.

WALK 9

HOB HURST'S HOUSE AND GIBBET MOOR

DIFFICULTY  **DISTANCE 6 miles (9.6 km)**

HELL BANK PLANTATION — GIBBET MOOR — UMBERLEY BROOK — UMBERLEY WELL — HARLAND EDGE — RAVEN TOR — FALLINGE EDGE — HELL BANK PLANTATION

MAP OS Explorer OL24, The Peak District – White Peak area

STARTING POINT Hell Bank Plantation, on the minor road between Beeley and Holymoorside (GR 287681)

PARKING Beside the road

PUBLIC TRANSPORT None

Although a concessionary path negotiated with the Chatsworth Estate has enabled walkers to visit Hob Hurst's House for several years, the vast expanse of Gibbet Moor and Brampton East Moor, crossed by ancient trails, has been out of bounds. This walk also takes in newly accessible Fallinge Edge, above Beeley.

▶ Start the walk from the limited parking spaces at Hell Bank Plantation, where the minor road from Beeley comes out on to Beeley Moor at spot height 293 m on the map. Follow the walled track northwards to a stile giving access to the concessionary path that leads north on the open moor, crossing Harland Sick by a footbridge.

■ Beeley Moor is littered with prehistoric remains under the rough moorgrass, heather and bracken. Close to the path are enclosures, stone circles, tumuli and cairns all dating from the Bronze Age, indicating that these moorland shelves were home to settled farming communities up to 4000 years ago.

▶ The path leads up by the side of the southern end of Bunker's Hill Wood towards the enclosure at the top of the rise which surrounds the Bronze Age tumulus (burial mound) known as Hob Hurst's House ❶.

■ Hob Hurst's House is one of the most important of the Bronze Age tumuli found in the Peak, unusual because it is surrounded by an almost square ditch and embankment. Like so many of the Peak District's barrows, it features a large hole in the top, evidence of the work of Thomas Bateman, who excavated the mound in 1853. There is an interpretive plaque to explain the importance of the monument (see pages 113–14).

▶ The route now heads north on the track which leads along the western edge of heather-clad Gibbet Moor, keeping close to the edge of Bunker's Hill Wood on the left.

■ Gibbet Moor probably takes its name from the location of a gibbet in days gone by. The fate of criminals convicted of serious crimes such as murder was a grim one: they would be executed, usually by hanging, and the body would be placed in an iron cage, which was then strung up on a post and left to rot – a gruesome example to others.

▶ Follow the enclosure wall across Gibbet Moor to a track which leads down to the valley of the Umberley Brook and the access point on the A619 Baslow–Chesterfield road, east of the Robin Hood pub ❷.
  Now head south up the valley of the Umberley Brook, crossing the conduit which supplies water to the Emperor Lake in the woods behind Chatsworth House. Keep to the right (west)

bank of the stream as it crosses the barren moor and follow it for a rough mile (1.6 km) until you reach the head of the stream at Umberley Well, where a number of ancient hollow ways cross near a guide stoop on the former route between Chesterfield and Bakewell (GR 288697) ❸.

■ The stoop (see pages 106–7) was a marker to show travellers crossing the featureless moor that they were on the correct route. With the representation of a hand pointing the way, the lettering confirms the 'Cheste-rfeild Road' and the 'Bakewe-ll Road' in incised characters. Near by, a stone slab bridge crosses the stream. There is another guide stoop with similar lettering about 350 yards (350 m) east of Hob Hurst's House (GR 287692).

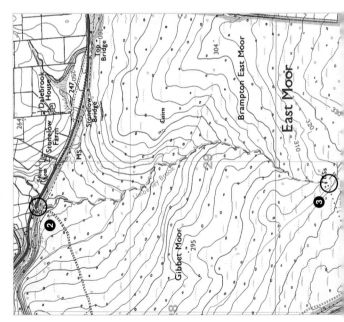

▶ Head south towards Hob Hurst's House again, and for a shorter walk return on your outward route to Hell Bank. Otherwise, bear left along the gritstone escarpment of Harland Edge ❹, which is a good spot to watch out for moorland birds of prey such as the hen harrier.

Where the edge peters out and joins the minor road coming up from Holymoorside, there is another guide stoop at the crossroads of routes between Bakewell ('Back-well'), Wirksworth ('Work-swor-th'), Chesterfield ('Che-stt-erf-eld') and Sheffield ('She-feld'). This interesting stoop lay buried for over fifty years until it was unearthed and re-erected by members of the Holymoorside Historical Society in 1995.

Turn right at the road and right again along the minor road which leads below Harland Edge, turning left on to a track which heads out into the heather of the moor. Where the track turns sharply left,

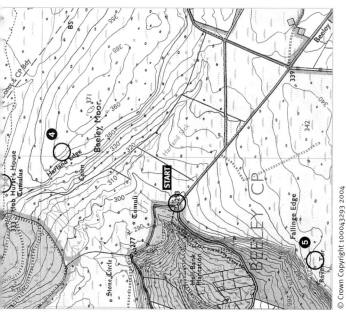

© Crown Copyright 100043293 2004

111

keep on straight across the heather heading for Raven Tor on Fallinge Edge (GR 282671) **5**, a fine viewpoint across Beeley village and the valley of the River Derwent, with the conifers of Lindop Wood beyond.

It is now a short, if rough, step right (north) along Fallinge Edge, back to the start at Hell Bank.

Leaving Beeley Moor, with Harland Edge in the background

Hob-nobbing with the spirits

Hob Hurst's House, the remote Bronze Age burial mound 1000 ft (305 m) up on Brampton East Moor, was excavated in June 1853 by the indefatigable barrow digger, Thomas Bateman. In one of his most evocative descriptions of the opening of a barrow, he wrote how he discovered a deposit of calcined human bones 'lying in the very spot where they had been drawn together while the embers of the funeral pyre were glowing'.

But why did the barrow acquire the name Hob Hurst's House? In his classic *Ten Years' Diggings in Celtic & Saxon Grave Hills* (1861), Bateman attempted to give an explanation:

> In the popular name given to the barrow, we have an indirect testimony to its great antiquity, as Hobhurst's House signifies the abode of an unearthly or supernatural being, accustomed to haunt woods and other solitary places, respecting whom many traditions yet linger in remote villages. Such an idea could only arise in a superstitious age long ago, yet sufficiently modern to have effaced all traditionary recollection of the original intention of the mound; it likewise affords a curious instance of the inherent tendency of the mind to assign a reason for everything uncommon or unaccountable, which no extent of ignorance or apathy seems able totally to eradicate.

According to folklore, Hob or Hob I' th' Hurst was a mischievous wood elf or fairy (the word 'hurst' comes from the Old English for a wood or forest). Hobgoblin comes from the same source. As in many other remote places, belief in such ephemeral beings existed until well into the nineteenth century and even later.

Hob was thought to inhabit ancient stone circles and burial mounds or even natural features such as prominent rock outcrops or caves, and he is commemorated in a number of Peak District names. Hob's House can be found on the slopes of Fin Cop, above the River Wye near Ashford; Thurst House Cave is in Deep Dale, near King's Sterndale; and Hob Tor is the name given to an outcrop above Dove Holes, north of Buxton.

Local people would be loath to visit these lonely places at certain times, such as after dark, for fear of upsetting such a capricious creature. If you did, your cows would go dry, the milk would turn sour, the cream wouldn't churn into butter and the hay crop would fail. Worse than that, Hob might also turn into a poltergeist and begin to throw crockery about the farmhouse.

On the other hand, if you kept Hob on your side he would ensure that everything ran smoothly on the farm. Your cows would give plenty of milk, the cream would churn easily and your hay crop would provide sufficient feed to see your stock through the long, cold winter.

WALK 10

ELDON HILL AND HOLE

DIFFICULTY 👢 👢 **DISTANCE About 5 miles (8 km)**

PEAK FOREST   ELDON HOLE   ELDON HILL   OLD MOOR   OXLOW RAKE   PEAK FOREST

MAPS OS Explorer OL24, The Peak District – White Peak area;
OS Explorer OL1, The Peak District – Dark Peak area

STARTING POINT Peak Forest (GR 113792)

PARKING In the village

PUBLIC TRANSPORT Buses from Sheffield and
Chapel-en-le-Frith

This walk takes you to the top and bottom of the White Peak. The rolling hills, such as Eldon Hill to the north of Peak Forest, are the highest in the Peak's limestone country, and Eldon Hole – one of the original Seven Wonders of the Peak – was long thought to be bottomless. Both are visited on this easy, half-day walk.

▶ The walk starts at the village of Peak Forest on the busy A623 Baslow–Chapel-en-le-Frith road.

■ Peak Forest stands at the heart of what was once the Royal Forest of the Peak, and Chamber Farm, to the west of the village, is thought to have been the site of Swainmote Court, where offenders who broke the strict forest laws were dealt with by the Steward of the Forest.

The Royal Forest of the Peak was a 40-square-mile (100-sq-km) royal hunting ground between the Wye and Etherow rivers, and was originally administered from Peveril Castle. The conies, or rabbits, of the forest are still remembered in the names of Conies Dale and Conies Farm to the north of the village.

Peak Forest's parish church, founded in 1657, is unusually dedicated to 'King Charles the Martyr'. By a quirk of ecclesiastical law, the minister here had the power to issue marriage licences from 1665 until the passing of the Marriage Act in 1753, and many runaway marriages were performed, making this the Peak's Gretna Green. One of these couples was the unfortunate Allan and Clara, who were murdered in the Winnats Pass at Castleton in 1758. Although not strictly legal, the custom survived despite the change in the law until around 1804.

▶ From the crossroads in the centre of the village opposite the church, walk north into Church Lane leading to the hamlet of

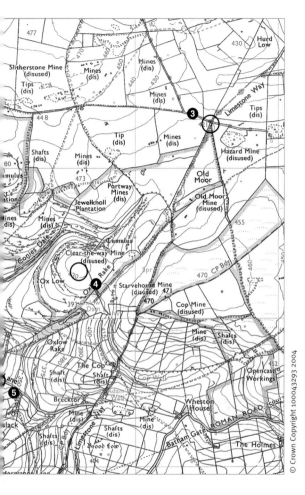

© Crown Copyright 100043293 2004

Old Dam. Turn left at the road junction, and then right at Eldon Lane End Farm into Eldon Lane. The lane becomes a track which rises to a stile and continues to ascend gradually beside a wall.

Just past an old lead rake marked by a line of trees on

your left, a path runs above the rake towards the gaping, tree-lined pothole of Eldon Hole ❶.

■ Eldon Hole is the largest open pothole in the Peak. As one of the original Seven Wonders of the Peak (see pages 121–2), it was a place of dread and fear to locals, and many are the tales of people being lowered into it and coming out as white-haired, gibbering idiots.

Charles Cotton, the seventeenth-century translator of *Wonders of the Peake*, claimed he had let out 800 fathoms (4800 ft/ 1463 m) of line into it without finding the bottom – but his rope probably just coiled up when it reached the bottom of the shaft. When Eldon Hole was eventually descended for the first time by John Lloyd in 1780, it was found to be only 269 ft (82 m) deep, with a number of other chambers leading off it.

▶ From Eldon Hole, it is a short step up the grassy slopes to

reach the summit of Eldon Hill (GR 115811) at 1543 ft (470 m) ❷, one of the highest limestone hills in the Peak. The honour of being the highest falls to the rounded hill across the shallow valley to the north-east of Eldon, now un-named but known on the first-edition OS map as The Beet,

which stands at 1565 ft (477 m). Unfortunately, there is still no access to this actual summit of the White Peak.

■ Eldon Hill, now open to access for the first time, commands extensive views towards the Great Ridge and Mam Tor, and south across the rolling White Peak plateau. Its name means 'elves hill', but for many years the 'elves' of Eldon were the quarrymen who blasted away the whole of the western side of the hill in their quest for aggregate limestone. This

An early expedition to Eldon Hole

ugly quarry was dubbed by conservationists 'the worst eyesore in the Peak' and the National Park authority fought a twenty-year battle to close it down, eventually succeeding in 1995. The site has been restored with extensive tree planting, now in the after-care phase.

▶ From Eldon Hill summit, retrace your steps to join the path climbing over the northern shoulder of the hill and reach a gate on to a broad walled lane.

Go right along the lane and continue eastwards through a landscape pitted by generations of lead miners. The descriptively named Slitherstone mine is on the hillside to your left.

Just after the metalled lane leading left towards Rowter Farm, turn right on the Limestone Way ❸, following a broken-down wall south across Old Moor to a gate. Continue down the lane with Oxlow Rake to your right. The rounded hill is Ox Low ❹, with the remains of the Clear-the-way lead mine on its craggy northern slopes and the shallow, dry depression of Conies Dale

beyond. The limestone scars or outcrops of Conies Dale are typical of the open, uninhabited waste which was once the Royal Forest of the Peak.

Passing through three further stiles, you cross a farm track and take the stile in the wall opposite, veering left now to reach Old Dam Lane again ❺. The tumulus-topped hill opposite is Snelslow, today clothed in a plantation.

■ Snelslow Plantation (GR 119794) is an award-winning example of woodland management undertaken by the National Park authority. It thinned this exposed hilltop wood and replanted it in a scheme which won a Centre of Excellence award from the forestry authority. One enterprising young forester even managed to create a wooden sculpture using his chain saw in the heart of the plantation.

▶ Turn right here to walk back to Church Lane, turning left to re-enter Peak Forest.

The Seven Wonders
of the Peak

Many of the early travellers to the Peak District came in search of the fabled Seven Wonders of the Peak, a seventeenth-century device designed to attract visitors and to reflect the Seven Wonders of the Ancient World.

They were first described by Michael Drayton, the popular Tudor poet, in the third edition of his *Poly-Olbion or a Chorographicall Description of Tracts, Rivers, Mountaines, Forests, and other Parts of this Renowned Isle of Great Britaine*, published in 1622. The Seven Wonders soon became part of the grand tour of the area undertaken by travellers from the south, such as the cynical journalist and author of *Robinson Crusoe* Daniel Defoe and the intrepid side-saddle rider, Celia Fiennes.

The wonders as Drayton described them were: the Devil's Arse (Peak Cavern at Castleton), Poole's Hole (Poole's Cavern at Buxton), Eldon Hole (visited in Walk 10), Saint Anne's Well at Buxton, the Ebbing and Flowing Well at Tydeswell (at Tideswell or Barmoor Clough, near Chapel-en-le-Frith), Sandy Hill (Mam Tor, near Castleton) and the hunting preserve of the Royal Forest of the Peak.

Peak Cavern had always been known as the Devil's Arse before Victorian sensibilities sanitized its name, and Peakshole Water which runs out from it was thought by local people to be evidence of the Devil relieving himself. A goose which was dropped down the Peak's biggest open pothole at Eldon Hole, to find out where it led, was said to have emerged several days later through the massive entrance of Peak Cavern – the largest natural cave entrance in Britain – having had its feathers singed en route by its apparent passage through the fires of Hell. Daniel Defoe, in his *Tour through the Whole Island of Great Britain*

(1724–26), thought the 'frightful chasm' of Eldon Hole was the only natural wonder worth the name among the so-called Wonders of the Peak.

St Anne's Well at Buxton probably takes its name from Arn or Anu, a Celtic goddess after whom the Romans originally named the spa town Aquae Arnemetiae. And the name of Mam Tor, standing proudly at the head of the Hope valley and ringed by the impressive embankments of a late Bronze Age hill fort, probably has a similar Celtic origin and is thought to mean 'mother mountain'.

Drayton's wonders were later adopted, with the replacement of the medieval royal forest by Chatsworth House, by the philosopher Thomas Hobbes in his *De Mirabilibus Pecci: Concerning the Wonders of the Peak in Darby-shire*, published in long-winded Latin hexameters in 1636. This was an astute move by Hobbes because he was at the time the tutor to the Cavendish children at Chatsworth.

Charles Cotton of Beresford Hall in Dovedale, co-author with Izaak Walton of the fisherman's bible, *The Compleat Angler*, later translated Hobbes's Latin into English, and cleverly had his *Wonders of the Peake* (1681) published to great acclaim in the surrounding towns and cities, from where most visitors to the Peak came and still come.

A modern list of Wonders of the Peak would probably include some of the amazing natural features of the Dark Peak moors, which were so abhorrent to travellers of the seventeenth century, such as Kinder Downfall, the Wool Packs, Alport Castles and the tors of Bleaklow.

WALK 11

THE MANIFOLD AND ECTON

DIFFICULTY 👢 👢   **DISTANCE About 6 miles (9.6 km)**

| HULME END | ECTON HILL | WETTON HILLS | WETTON MILL | SWAINSLEY | MANIFOLD TRACK | HULME END |

MAP OS Explorer OL24, The Peak District – White Peak area

STARTING POINT Hulme End (GR 102593)

PARKING At Hulme End

PUBLIC TRANSPORT Infrequent bus service and occasional Postbus to Leek

New access legislation has opened up Ecton Hill, site of a lucrative copper mine owned by the Duke of Devonshire during the eighteenth century, and the twin Wetton Hills, its southern neighbours, on the eastern banks of the disappearing River Manifold. This easy walk links the three hills, returning via the Manifold Track.

▶ The walk starts from Hulme End, the northern terminus of the former Leek and Manifold Light Railway, now the Manifold Track walking and riding route.

■ The Leek and Manifold Light Railway was one of the most romantic yet short-lived of the Peak's railways. It opened in 1904 to serve the copper mines at Ecton Hill (see pages 130–31) and to take out mainly dairy products from the scattered farming communities west of Hartington. The line used rolling stock and engines salvaged from India, and was famous for its primrose-yellow carriages which wound along the scenic Manifold valley with tiny stations at places like Thor's Cave and Beeston Tor. But it was always doomed to failure because, as a local remarked, 'it starts from nowhere and finishes up at the same place'. The line closed after just thirty years in 1934.

In a pioneering move by Staffordshire County Council in 1937, the former trackbed was converted to a popular walking and riding route known as the Manifold Track.

▶ Follow the track south to Dale Bridge passing Apes Tor on your left, one of several quarried crags of reef limestone which mark the length of the Manifold valley, and the site of another former copper mine. Turn left on to the minor road which leads steeply up towards the green copper-spired building known as Radcliffe's Folly, a fairy-tale Gothic structure built by local MP Arthur Radcliffe in the 1930s ❶.

Through the archway take the stile which leads off up to the left and ascend the slopes below the horseshoe-shaped conifer plantation which covers spoil from the Dutchman mine. There are now increasingly fine views west down the wooded Manifold valley and towards Warslow on the plateau above.

You will soon come across more remains from the Ecton copper mines, including the former engine house which sheltered a Boulton & Watt beam engine installed to drain the mine in 1788 and which had to

have its roof lowered in 1924 because it lost so many tiles in the high Staffordshire winds. You also pass the former sales office and mine agent's house and several deep shafts, such as the Deep Ecton, which, although fenced, should still be approached with extreme care. There are thought to be about seventy mine workings scattered over the hill, including no less than forty to fifty vertical shafts.

■ The Ecton copper mines were worked for well over three centuries, and there is increasing archaeological evidence to show that they were also worked in prehistoric times. Their boom period was between 1760 and 1818, when Ecton had the deepest mine in Britain.

▶ Now in newly opened access country, you can head directly for the summit of Ecton Hill (GR 100580) at 1211 ft (369 m) ❷, with extensive views westwards down across Swainsley and up the valley of the Warslow Brook, towards the distant whaleback of Morridge on the skyline. Below

you to the east are the remains of further copper and lead mines, such as the Clayton Pipe and the Chadwick mine.

Descend to a gate, turning left alongside a wall to the access road to Broad Ecton Farm. Follow the walled lane south down into the dale to the road end in the area known as Back of Ecton. Keep on this walled track as it descends past Lees Farm and Manor House on the left, to the building at the road end formerly known as the Pepper Inn ❸.

■ The Pepper Inn has a varied history. It was built in the eighteenth century as an alehouse for miners from Ecton, and later was used as a smallpox isolation hospital and a button factory.

▶ Take the footbridge over the stream at the foot of Wetton Hill, which now rises steeply in front of you. The easiest route of ascent is to follow the footpath which heads to the col between the twin summits (National Trust). It is a short step right from here to reach the tumulus-topped summit of Wetton Hill (west) at 1174 ft

(358 m) ❹, and to enjoy a fine view westward across the deep trench of the Manifold valley and south across the village of Wetton in the valley below.

Summit-baggers will want also to take in the eastern and higher summit of the Wetton Hills (GR 113566), at 1217 ft (371 m) ❺, and a view which extends east towards Narrowdale Hill, with Gratton Hill to the right and the distant trench of Wolfscote Dale at the northern end of Dovedale.

■ Aptly named Narrowdale, which leads down to the village of Alstonefield, and its tumulus-topped, open-access hill (GR 123573), has the distinction of an entry in Brewer's *Dictionary of Phrase and Fable*. Apparently to postpone a matter 'till Narrowdale noon' meant to defer it indefinitely. The saying came about because of the narrowness of the dale where, according to the story, residents did not see the sun for half the year.

▶ Retrace your steps to the western Wetton Hill summit, and then drop down the steep, grassy slopes to a little nameless valley and the path which runs south-west through a rock cutting leading down to Wetton Mill ❻.

■ Wetton Mill is an attractive hamlet grouped around Wetton Mill Bridge, which was rebuilt by the Duke of Devonshire in 1807 to serve his copper-mining interests at Ecton Hill. The mill itself was a grist mill used by local farmers until 1857, when it closed. All this area is part of the National Trust's South Peak Estate, and it was the trust which provided the café and toilet facilities at the car park at Wetton Mill. The crag of Nan Tor, above the café, has caves which have revealed evidence of mesolithic hunter-gatherers some 8500 years ago.

The River Manifold exhibits that eccentricity of some limestone rivers in that for most of the summer it disappears underground to run in fissures in the rock. In the case of the Manifold, this disappearing act happens at Wetton Mill and the river follows an underground course for over 3 miles (4.8 km) until it bubbles to the surface again in the grounds of Ilam Hall at the southern end of Dovedale.

▶ Now follow the old gated road from Dale Farm which contours north following the course of the River Manifold just above its flood plain, occasionally passing through delightful woodland and reaching the hamlet of Swainsley after about a mile (1.6 km) **7**.

■ The circular dovecote seen across the river just as you approach Swainsley was built by the owners of nearby Swainsley Hall in the nineteenth century. Apparently pigeons still use the charming building, which at one time was also used as a fishing temple, a shelter 'sacred' to anglers.

▶ Walk over Ecton Bridge and immediately turn right at the stile which leads to a path crossing Warslow Brook and joining the Manifold Track. The line of the former railway is now followed as it twists and turns northwards with the valley for just over a mile (1.6 km). Over to your right you will soon see the green spire of Radcliffe's Folly and the remaining buildings of the mine. Passing under Apes Tor, you are soon back to the starting point at Hulme End.

The Manifold valley

Copper-bottomed success

Visitors to Chatsworth and the elegant Crescent in Buxton may not realize it, but much of the wealth which enabled the Dukes of Devonshire to build these magnificent structures was founded on the extraordinary profits made from their mineral workings at Ecton Hill in the Manifold valley.

Best known for its huge reserves of high-quality copper, the hill also produced marketable quantities of lead and zinc at a time when these minerals were in demand for the plumbing and roofing of the great houses constructed during the age of rebuilding in the seventeenth and eighteenth centuries. It has been estimated that about 100,000 tons of ore were taken from these hills, the majority of which were high-quality copper (fifteen per cent pure) obtained by the Duke of Devonshire during the eighteenth century.

Recent archaeological research has proved that the mineral reserves of Ecton were known and used in prehistoric times. The finding of antler tools and hammer stones in old workings close to the surface seems to indicate that the underground riches of this Staffordshire hill were well known to the first metal-workers.

Commercial working started in the seventeenth century, and by the later years of that century Ecton had become one of the first mines in the country to use gunpowder to get to the precious ore. Dr Robert Plot in his *Natural History of Staffordshire* (1686) mentions in his description of the mine, 'they broke the rocks with Gunpowder and got 3 sorts of Ore: 1. a black sort which was best, 2. a yellow sort, the worst, and 3. a mixt sort of both'.

In 1723, the third Duke of Devonshire granted a lease to eight 'adventurers' from Derbyshire and Staffordshire to work the mine for twenty-one years. The lease was later renewed with other businessmen, and the scene was set for Ecton Hill's most productive period, when it became one of the richest copper mines in Britain. Between 1760 and 1817 some 66,000 tons of copper ore were extracted, worth £852,000 and yielding a profit of £335,000. This was an astronomical figure for those days – an average profit of £6,000 a year.

The biggest shaft at Ecton was the Deep Ecton, which when sunk in 1795 was 924 ft (282 m) below the surface, and the deepest in Britain. By 1840, the shaft had reached about 1300 ft (396 m) in depth. The awesome Water Engine Shaft in Ecton Deep Adit is now filled with water, which is no longer being pumped out, and is 600 ft (183 m) deep. The miners, who often doubled as farmers, built an entire subterranean town beneath the surface, with blacksmiths' shops and other workshops to serve the excavations.

Ecton continued to be worked, with varying degrees of success, throughout the nineteenth century, but finally closed in 1888, in the face of increased flooding of the shafts and the apparent exhaustion of easily obtainable ore.

WALK 12

THE PEAKS OF THE UPPER DOVE

DIFFICULTY  DISTANCE 6 miles (9.6 km)

LONGNOR   CHROME   DOWEL   HIGH   LONGNOR
            HILL   DALE   WHEELDON
    PARKHOUSE   OWL   EARL   BEGGAR'S
    HILL   HOLE   STERNDALE   BRIDGE

MAP OS Explorer OL24, The Peak District – White Peak area

STARTING POINT Longnor

PARKING In Market Square car park (GR 088649)

PUBLIC TRANSPORT Buses to Buxton and Hartington, and
infrequently to Leek

The reef limestone hills of Parkhouse, Chrome and High Wheeldon are among the only true 'peaks' in the Peak District. This walk around the hills of the upper Dove valley visits all three of them.

▶ The walk starts from the cobbled Market Square of Longnor, the gritstone village which sits on the ridge between the upper valleys of the Dove and Manifold.

■ The gabled nineteenth-century Market Hall, now a craft centre, at Longnor still has a sign showing the scale of tolls for traders on its wall. Longnor once stood at the junction of a number of important turnpike roads which crossed the Staffordshire moors, and Longnor people are keen to point out that the postal address of the nearby town of Leek was once 'near Longnor' – not the other way around.

▶ From Market Square walk up the little alleyway of Chapel Street, across Church Street and into a lane. Follow the footpath sign (right) and the wall up the hill to reach a stile and a fine viewpoint across the valley to the hills of the upper Dove.

■ The upstanding hills of the upper Dove were formed around 350 million years ago, under conditions very similar to those that exist today on the Great Barrier Reef off the eastern coast of Australia. At that time, Britain was much closer to the Equator, and this area was submerged under a warm, shallow tropical sea.

On the edge of this warm sea, coral reefs built up, eventually to form the more resistant limestone from which the present Chrome, Parkhouse and High Wheeldon hills are created. The sharp defile of Dowel

Dale across the valley is thought to have been an underwater inter-reef channel, and so to have been there since the hills were built up. This very hard reef limestone is also responsible for the famous pinnacles and crags of the lower reaches of Dovedale downstream.

▶ Follow the path which heads down the bank to join a farm track leading to Yew Tree Grange, to reach the road junction with the B5053. Turn right here and just before the road starts a sharp descent to Glutton Bridge ❶, turn left on the lane to Dove Bank and through two stiles to reach a footbridge over the Dove. You now join the minor road leading up into Dowel Dale, turning left under the serrated shadow of Parkhouse Hill at 1221 ft (372 m) ❷ with its attendant sharply pointed outlier known as the Sugar Loaf.

There is now access to the summit of Parkhouse Hill above you to the right. But the ascent of Parkhouse Hill is really for experienced scramblers and climbers only, and the traverse of its sharply jagged and rocky ridge requires the use of hands and a very good head for heights. Sufferers from vertigo are advised not to attempt it.

Just past the Sugar Loaf, you will see a sign on your left pointing out the footpath which gives access to the fine ridge walk crossing Chrome Hill – locally and appropriately known as the Dragon's Back. Follow the ridge up the steep grassy slopes to a stile by a stately sycamore tree, with outstanding views back down the valley of the Dove and across the slightly lower, but no less impressive, pinnacled ridge of Parkhouse Hill.

■ Chrome Hill, at 1411 ft (430 m), is pronounced 'croom' and is thought to have taken its unusual name from the Old English word for curved or sickle-shaped. This is a perfect description of its curving summit ridge, which provides one of the finest ridge walks in the Peak District. If you stick to the actual crest all the way you will need a good head for heights, as the ridge weaves

© Crown Copyright 100043293 2004

and dips between limestone outcrops. There is an easy and less vertiginous alternative path on the northern side.

The view from the summit (GR 072673) ❸ is outstanding, extending as far as Axe Edge to the west and the dim outline of Kinder Scout beyond Buxton to the north. Nearer at hand are the Dove and neighbouring Manifold valleys, while there is an almost aerial view of the tiny hamlet of Hollinsclough directly below.

▶ At the northernmost end of the ridge, a waymark points to a path which skirts a walled enclosure, with Tor Rock upstanding to the right. Passing through an old wall and several stiles, you reach the drive to Stoops Farm and the junction with the Dowel Dale road opposite High Edge. Turn right on this unfenced road and walk past Greensides to drop down into Dowel Dale, with the fenced open pothole known as Owl Hole ❹ on the left.

■ The steep-sided Dowel Dale was deepened by a glacial meltwater stream which joined the Dove between Chrome and Parkhouse Hills. At the foot of the dale, in the cliffs opposite Dowall Hall, the shallow Dowel Cave has revealed evidence of paleolithic (early Stone Age) occupation perhaps 20,000 years ago, when it was used by hunting parties seeking out game in the surrounding hills.

▶ At the head of Dowel Dale ❺, just before it turns to the south, take the stile on the left and the path which leads uphill steeply and then more easily. The path crosses a farm track and then leads into another, continuing down to the minor road near Harley Grange. Turn right here and walk down, crossing the Longnor–Buxton road and into the village of Earl Sterndale ❻.

■ Earl Sterndale, with its limestone cottages, got its name from William de Ferrars, Earl of Derby, who held the estate in 1244. The village clusters around its small green, and is perhaps most famous for its welcoming pub with the unusual name of The Quiet Woman. Why she is quiet is obvious from the signboard – she has no head! The story is that a former landlord was so fed up with his nagging wife that he decapitated her. The refurbished church of St Michael's contains a twelfth-century font, and was the unfortunate victim of a stray German bomb during the Second World War.

▶ Follow the village street leading south-east, and then the minor road which branches off right past a small dewpond (locally known as a mere) towards Abbotside Farm and the old quarry beneath Alderley Cliff. A National Trust sign opposite the quarry leads to a stile and a path which ascends steeply beside a dry-stone wall towards the conical summit of High Wheeldon ❼. This is reached by a path coming up from Wheeldon Trees on the left, past the ruins of a lime kiln.

■ At 1383 ft (422 m), the long ridge of High Wheeldon is another of the finest viewpoints in the White Peak, taking in much of the route of this walk and including the splendid peaks of the upper Dove.

Just below the summit to the north-east is the locked entrance to Fox Hole Cave, where paleolithic and neolithic remains have been discovered in a fissure-type chamber 180 ft (54 m) long.

▶ Turn south from the summit and follow the path which leads steeply down to a wall, turning right where it meets another wall and contours down to the road to Crowdicote. Turn left on this and then right on to the unsurfaced walled Green Lane, which leads down to Beggar's Bridge ❽ across the River Dove.

From the bridge, the footpath crosses ancient ridge-and-furrow cultivations before climbing to a gate near a barn. Bear left for the final climb of the day to Top o' th' Edge and a walled lane that leads back to Longnor. Turn right to regain the centre of the village.

The upper Dove valley, showing Chrome (centre) and Parkhouse (right)

Some further reading

Here is a small selection of books which will tell you more about the area. Please note that not all of them are still in print.

Anon., *Freedom of the Moors*, Sheffield Campaign for Access to Moorland, 1988

John Barnatt and Ken Smith, *The Peak District: Landscapes through Time*, Windgather Press, 2004

Rex Bellamy, *The Peak District Companion*, David & Charles, 1981

Bill Bevan, *The Upper Derwent*, Tempus, 2004

Roger Dalton, Howard Fox and Peter Jones, *Classic Landforms of the Dark Peak*, The Geographical Association, 1999

John Derry, *Across the Derbyshire Moors*, Loxley Bros, 1904

Howard Hill, *Freedom to Roam*, Moorland, 1980

Terence M. Howard, *A Moorland Notebook*, Sheffield Campaign for Access to Moorland, n.d.

Roy Millward and Adrian Robinson, *The Peak District*, Eyre Methuen, 1975

John Pemberton, *Tom Tomlinson of Hathersage*, Nottinghamshire County Council, 1997

Lindsey Porter and John Robey, *The Copper & Lead Mines around the Manifold Valley*, Landmark, 2000

Mark Richards, *White Peak Walks – the Southern Dales*, Cicerone, 1988

Brian Robinson, *Memories of Tin Town*, J.W. Northend, n.d.

Neville T. Sharpe, *Crosses of the Peak District*, Landmark, 2002

David Sissons (ed.), *The Best of the Sheffield Clarion Ramblers' Handbooks*, Halsgrove, 2002

Howard Smith, *The Guide Stoops of the Dark Peak*, Howard Smith, 2000

Roland Smith, *First and Last*, Peak Park Joint Planning Board, 1978

Roly Smith, *Peak District: Collins Rambler's Guide*, HarperCollins, 2000

Roly Smith, *Murder and Mystery in the Peak*, Halsgrove, 2004

Roly Smith, *The Peak District: Official National Park Guide*, Pevensey (David & Charles), 2000

The Country Code

An abbreviated version of the Country Code, launched in 2004 and supported by a wide range of countryside organizations including the Ramblers' Association, is given below.

Be safe – plan ahead and follow signs

Even when going out locally, it's best to get the latest information about where and when you can go; for example, your rights to enter some areas of open land may be restricted while work is being carried out, for safety reasons or during breeding seasons. Follow advice and local signs, and be prepared for the unexpected.

Leave gates and property as you find them

Please respect the working life of the countryside, as our actions can affect rural livelihoods, the safety and welfare of animals and people, and the heritage that belongs to all of us.

Protect plants and animals, and take your litter home

We have a responsibility to protect the countryside now and for future generations, so make sure you don't harm animals, birds, plants or trees.

Keep dogs under control

The countryside is a great place to exercise dogs, but it's every owner's duty to make sure their dog is not a danger or nuisance to farm animals, wildlife or other people.

Consider other people

Showing consideration and respect for other people makes the countryside a pleasant environment for everyone, whether they are at home, at work or at leisure.

Index

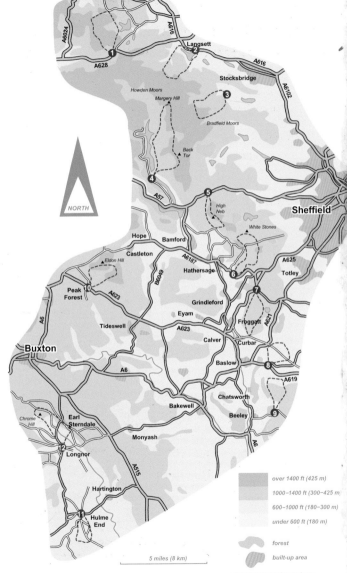

NORTH

A6024

A628

A616

1

2 Langsett

A616

Stocksbridge

A6102

Howden Moors

Margery Hill

3

Bradfield Moors

Back Tor

4

A57

5

High Neb

Sheffield

White Stones

Hope   Bamford

Castleton

Eldon Hill

A6187

Hathersage

A625

6

Totley

Peak Forest

10

A623

B6049

Grindleford

7

Tideswell

Eyam

Froggatt

A621

A623

Calver

Curbar

Buxton

A6

Baslow

8

A619

Chatsworth

Bakewell

Beeley

9

Chrome Hill

Earl Sterndale

A6

12

Longnor

Monyash

A515

Hartington

11 Hulme End

over 1400 ft (425 m)

1000–1400 ft (300–425 m)

600–1000 ft (180–300 m)

under 600 ft (180 m)

forest

built-up area

5 miles (8 km)

Not all minor roads are shown